"In *Tomorrow Needs You*, Naeem Fazal takes through his own life, showing us how fear and faith often intersect in our lives. His candor and transparency remind us that sometimes our greatest fears can be like those really bad haircuts—we just need to grow through them to find our true strength. Naeem beautifully weaves together Scripture and deep spiritual insights, offering a road map for anyone ready to face their anxieties, shake hands with freedom, and embrace their God-given potential. *Tomorrow Needs You* is a must-read for anyone brave enough to confront their fears—and maybe even laugh at a few along the way."

Tim Timberlake, author of *The Art of Overcoming* and senior pastor of Celebration Church

"'Fear is a squatter.' 'Fear promises us self-preservation, but it does not tell us it will cause us to self-decay.' In *Tomorrow Needs You*, Naeem Fazal tackles the debilitating power of fear in our lives. He addresses the many layers and faces with which fear shows up to dim our presence in the present. His sincere voice and storytelling feel like the stretched-out hand of Jesus inviting us to be all he created us to be now, even in the midst of uncertainty."

Noemi Chavez, pastor at Revive Church in Long Beach, California, and cofounder of Brave Global

"Naeem has done it again! His first book, *Ex-Muslim*, was a jaw-dropping, fantastic story of a life completely transformed by the living Jesus. Now he lays out a narrative that every person, Christian and non-Christian, needs to read. Naeem guides us through the process of leaving past fears and failure in yesterday. Through biblical wisdom and heartfelt storytelling, he sketches out a road map into the unknown future of tomorrow. If you have ever thought you were not enough or struggled with the idea of being trapped in the baggage of your past, this book is for you. It's a must-read for anyone who is seeking forward steps in their faith and in their life. It rightfully deserves a place on everyone's bookshelf."

Craig Wendel, church planter and author of *The 5 1/2 Mile High Club* and *Warrior King*

"*Tomorrow Needs You* by Naeem Fazal is a powerful and captivating invitation to break free from the past and step boldly into the future. Through his personal stories—both natural and supernatural—Naeem skillfully shows how fear can keep us bound to old narratives, holding us back from a new tomorrow that cannot exist without us. This book encourages us to connect with the God who knows our future from our beginning, helping us access hope and seek beauty that overrides fear. As Naeem so beautifully reminds us, tomorrow needs us now!"

Lucretia Carter Berry, educator, author, and founder of Brownicity

"Most of us would probably say that we want to focus on the future instead of the past, but it is so easy to be trapped by yesterday. If that's where you find yourself, then you need my friend Naeem's book. God is calling each of us to step into a tomorrow that is better than anything we could have imagined. What's holding you back?"

Josh Surratt, lead pastor of Seacoast Church

"This book is a beautiful, layered journey of triumph and vulnerability. The author's willingness to share personal anecdotes creates a powerful connection with readers. I'm grateful for this early glimpse and excited for others to experience it. The underlying tone of hope and the framing of failures as God's pit stops—not meant to define us—transcend all faiths. This perspective empowers readers to offer themselves more grace. The book doesn't just inspire; it provides a transformative lens through which to view life's challenges. It's a testament to perseverance and the beauty of embracing our full journey, setbacks and all."

Ismail Badjie, founder and CEO of Innovarx Global Health

"In a refreshing departure from typical self-help books, *Tomorrow Needs You* offers something rare: relatability. Naeem's words push past the spiritual clichés that are often offered in dark moments of despair. Instead, he acknowledges your pain and sits with you in it. This just might be the book that finally helps you grasp how deeply God cares about every detail of your life, especially the ones where it's hard to see him. Naeem's unique style of compassion and inspiration is evident in the heartfelt stories he shares, inviting you to release the breath you didn't realize you were holding."

Kristin Mockler Young, pastor and host of *Becoming Church* podcast

"In *Tomorrow Needs You*, Naeem Fazal crafts a powerful, vivid narrative that resonates with the bold intensity of Van Gogh's art. With each page, Fazal invites readers to confront life's necessary endings and embrace a fresh canvas for the future—one painted with beauty, joy, purpose, and possibilities. This book provides for a transformative journey that will enrich your life, spark new relationships, and deepen your experience with Jesus."

Mark DeYmaz, founding pastor of Mosaic Church of Central Arkansas and author of *Disruption: Repurposing the Church to Redeem the Community*

"I'm thrilled to recommend Naeem Fazal's *Tomorrow Needs You*. This inspiring book addresses a universal enemy: fear. Naeem explores how fear manifests itself as worry and uncertainty, clouding our vision of a brighter future. He guides us to a life enriched by hope and perseverance, following Jesus' example. Naeem inspires us to embrace our dreams and become who we aspire to be by celebrating life's beauty despite challenges. If you're seeking inspiration and a fresh perspective on overcoming fear, this is a must-read!"

Jill Bjers, managing director at BrainBloom Labs and TEDx Charlotte curator

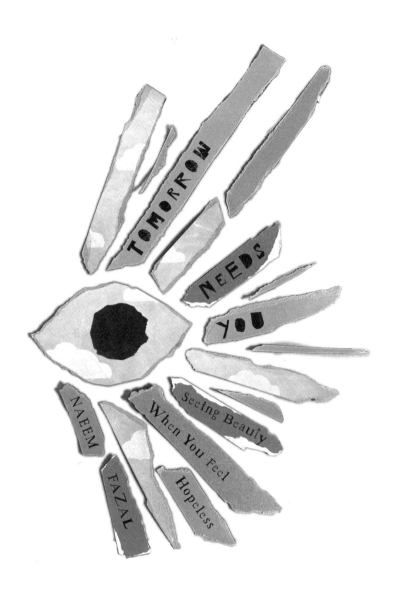

TOMORROW NEEDS YOU

Seeing Beauty When You Feel Hopeless

NAEEM FAZAL

Foreword by Derwin L. Gray

An imprint of InterVarsity Press
Downers Grove, Illinois

InterVarsity Press
P.O. Box 1400 | Downers Grove, IL 60515-1426
ivpress.com | email@ivpress.com

©2025 by Naeem Fazal

All rights reserved. No part of this book may be reproduced in any form without written permission from InterVarsity Press.

InterVarsity Press® is the publishing division of InterVarsity Christian Fellowship/USA®. For more information, visit intervarsity.org.

All Scripture quotations, unless otherwise indicated, are taken from The Holy Bible, New International Version®, NIV®. Copyright © 1973, 1978, 1984, 2011 by Biblica, Inc.™ Used by permission of Zondervan. All rights reserved worldwide. www.zondervan.com. The "NIV" and "New International Version" are trademarks registered in the United States Patent and Trademark Office by Biblica, Inc.™

While any stories in this book are true, some names and identifying information may have been changed to protect the privacy of individuals.

Published in association with The Bindery Agency, www.TheBinderyAgency.com.

The publisher cannot verify the accuracy or functionality of website URLs used in this book beyond the date of publication.

Cover design: Faceout Studio, Tim Green
Interior design: Daniel van Loon
Cover images: © Spiderstock / DigitalVision Vectors via Getty Images; © spaxiax / iStock / Getty Images Plus.
　　　　　　Paper Collage: Custom created by Faceout Studio, Tim Green; Clouds: GettyImages-157637579;
　　　　　　Background Texture: GettyImages-516634033

ISBN 978-1-5140-0988-8 (print) | ISBN 978-1-5140-0989-5 (digital)

Printed in the United States of America ∞

> **Library of Congress Cataloging-in-Publication Data**
> A catalog record for this book is available from the Library of Congress.

| 30 | 29 | 28 | 27 | 26 | 25 | | 12 | 11 | 10 | 9 | 8 | 7 | 6 | 5 | 4 | 3 | 2 | 1 |

Contents

Foreword by Derwin L. Gray *1*

Author's Note *3*

PART ONE: YESTERDAY HAS FORGOTTEN YOU *5*

1—Moving On *7*

2—Learning to Trust God Again *16*

PART TWO: TODAY IS WAITING *25*

3—My Relationship with Fear *27*

4—Fear of Loss *37*

5—Fear of Failure *45*

6—Fear of Rejection *54*

PART THREE: TOMORROW NEEDS YOU *63*

7—When Faith Fails *65*

8—Why Beauty? *73*

9—What Do You See? *80*

10—A Beautiful Vision *89*

11—A Beautiful Community *99*

12—A Beautiful Relationship *108*

13—The Broken Creating Beauty *117*

Acknowledgments *129*

Notes *133*

Foreword

DERWIN L. GRAY

NAEEM IS MY FRIEND. I have known him for nearly twenty years. He is a trophy of God's grace. He's had every reason to give up. He had a crippling learning disability that caused him to repeat fifth grade twice! He didn't think he was smart and neither did many of teachers. He knows the chaos and violence of war as Saddam Hussein's troops rolled into Kuwait. He knows the dehumanizing pain of racism in the Middle East and in America. Based on all the trauma Naeem has experienced, he shouldn't be a healthy, flourishing human, but Jesus has the final word, not our broken, sin-cursed world. Naeem embodies the apostle's words, "No, in all these things we are more than conquerors through him who loved us" (Romans 8:37 CSB).

Tomorrow Needs You is all about God's ability to take the broken pieces of our lives and create a beautiful mosaic of grace. Naeem's life displays how Jesus can pick up every shattered piece, every wound, every scar, and weave them together into a tapestry that showcases the goodness of God. Wounds become a testimony, and hurts become channels of healing. As you read his story, you'll find yourself encouraged, uplifted, and challenged to believe that God can do the same in your life.

Naeem has experienced deep loss, profound doubt, and unspeakable pain, but through it all, the Holy Spirit has called him past his fear into deeper faith. That's what makes his story so powerful. God took his pain and turned it into purpose. God took his past and gave him a future filled with hope. And that same God is reaching out to you through the pages of this book.

In *Tomorrow Needs You*, you will learn this simple but profound truth: everything that has happened will be redeemed. That's the promise we have in Jesus (Romans 8:28). God the Holy Spirit calls us past our fear into faith in Jesus. God takes our pain, our failures, our deepest wounds and turns them into platforms for purpose and conduits for healing. This is not just Naeem's story—it can be your story too.

So as you open this book, prepare to be challenged. Prepare to be inspired. And most importantly, prepare to meet the God who redeems all things. You are not too broken. Your past is not too far gone. And the pain you've experienced is not without purpose. Naeem's life is proof of that. God will redeem everything that has happened. He will take the broken pieces of your life and create something beautiful.

Friend, tomorrow needs you. And God is with you every step of the way.

Author's Note

Writing this book has been an emotional roller coaster. There were days that I was enthusiastically convinced that God had called and empowered me to do this. Then there were days my dyslexia and dysgraphia were in full effect, reminding me of my disability and triggering insecurities that I have struggled with my whole life. This book contains references to suicide and other traumatic experiences. It wrestles with darkness and discouragement as it finds the goodness of God and the power of his Spirit to be more than sufficient.

This book is dedicated to all of us who have ever felt paralyzed by our fears and failures. To all of us who have been through unimaginable trauma and pain. To all of us who are going through grief and despair. To all of us who have experienced the ugliness of this world.

But this book is also a declaration to our fears and failures, to our trauma and pain, and to our grief and despair—you will not imprison us.

Part One

Yesterday Has Forgotten You

Your past is too small for you to live in.

Yesterday has forgotten you, like someone you used to know. But have we broken up with yesterday? Yesterday was real. It happened. It was great for some of us and not so great for others of us. But answering this question is the first step of our journey to embrace today and look to our tomorrow.

We have to take the time to process and reconcile yesterday. It's understandable to linger in "what if" scenarios. I would love to change certain things in my past. Sometimes I think that if only I could change my past, my present would look different. But the truth is, looking at my past differently changes my present.

We have to appreciate, or perhaps grieve, our past. Otherwise, we will end up either repeating yesterday or becoming paralyzed today. That is why so many of us find ourselves in the same pattern of relationships and situations. There are different faces, different names, maybe even different places, but it's the same scenario again and again and again. Why is that? Because we haven't grieved and properly ended the relationship with yesterday.

And so, we are held captive by yesterday's voice. This negative inner voice reminds us of the hardest moments of our life, dragging us back into the memories. This voice is louder when we feel most helpless, and it convinces us that hope and love are too risky, so we hide. Before long, we are chained to insecurity and imprisoned by anxiety. The longer we are held captive to this voice, the more we are convinced we deserve to live this way. The more we listen and obey this voice, the more our worth withers away. But the truth is, the past is not thinking of us as much as we are thinking of it.

So, let's break up with yesterday.

One

Moving On

"It's about Dad," she said.

"What about Dad?"

She hesitated. I was at a tire shop replacing a flat tire. It had been one of those days—those days that start out okay and turn stressful by the hour. The day was almost over when I got the call.

"Dad is in the ER . . . He stabbed—"

She erupted into uncontrollable sobs. I could barely figure out what she was saying.

"He what?!" I asked nervously, raising my voice.

"He stabbed himself . . . He took a kitchen knife . . . The kids found him. He was just lying there, Naeem. Why did he do this? I don't understand why. Why would he do this? We just left him alone for an hour or so. Why did he do this? I can't believe it, Naeem."

"Okay, was he alive when you found him? Where is he now? Where was Mom? Is he stable?" I would have kept on asking questions, but I knew I needed to get there. My dad and mom were visiting my sister in Myrtle Beach, South Carolina. I was about four hours away in Charlotte, North Carolina—with a flat tire. I felt helpless.

"Okay, I'm on the way," I said as I ended the call.

My Dad's Story

The drive to the ER was rough. I was alone with my thoughts for four hours. I knew Dad had given up on life years ago. He began to believe he was unnecessary. It started when he moved to the United States. He was not this guy.

The dad I knew as I was growing up was ambitious and hard working. He was born in Pakistan, the youngest one of three brothers. He had half brothers because his dad, my grandfather, had two wives. (Muslims can legally have up to four wives.) But among all his brothers and sisters, Dad stood out. He never graduated from high school because at sixteen years old he jumped on a ship headed to Kuwait. He lied about how old he was and started working as soon as he got there.

Several years later he went back to Pakistan and married Mom, his first cousin. Marrying cousins is a common practice in Muslim cultures. In fact, in Dad's family, kids would be spoken for at an early age. My dad was one of three sons; his cousin (my mom) was one of three daughters. Each of the three sons married one of the three daughters. He eventually moved Mom to Kuwait, where most of my siblings and I were born and raised (my older brother was the only one of us born in Pakistan), and then later he sent us to the United States.

Dad continued to work in Kuwait to financially support us as we were trying to get settled in the States. In his thirty years in Kuwait, Dad worked his way up to management and then business partner, but eventually he left all that to come and be with us. At the time I thought it was the best thing for all of us. But, looking back, I am not sure it was.

Dad had swag. His fits were always on point. He also loved cool cars. I have a distinct memory of me, my brother, two sisters, and

Moving On 9

Mom all cramped into a sweet maroon two-door 1978 BMW 3-series coupe. That car did not last long; neither did the Audi coupe. I remember hearing about all his travels to Europe and China for business. Seeing photos of him standing beside the Great Wall of China, in European countries in the middle of real snow, and with white, blond people was thrilling for me as a kid. (Remember, I grew up in the desert.) I was about twelve years old when he gave me some money and encouraged me to go with friends to a fine-dining restaurant just for the experience. When I was growing up, my dad was the only one I knew who had flown on a Concorde, the supersonic commercial aircraft.

Dad was the most successful and generous of all his brothers. Growing up, I would hear stories about how he put my cousin through college in the United States. Although we were not rich, he provided for us to the point of figuring out a way to send his son to the States for college, and eventually helping us all migrate there.

Then disappointment changed him. He came to America and went from being a business partner to working at a convenience store and then doing odd jobs just trying to make money to help us. He came here after 9/11. We were all concerned about immigration policies, worried that they would eventually shut down access to Pakistanis coming to the States. So he came here—or, I should say, we made him come.

And then one day he had a heart attack, which ended up requiring him to have quadruple bypass surgery. After that, he never fully recovered. Even though physically he did, depression set in. He was different from then on: he refused to drive because he feared having a heart attack while he was on the road. Eventually his body began reacting to his emotional and psychological state. He began feeling unworthy and unnecessary. He saw us growing up and finding our own way. It did not help that now all of his kids had become Christians, leaving his Muslim faith behind. He was convinced that he had failed as a Muslim father.

He saw his kids marry and have kids, and now he was a grandfather. Yet he couldn't see the joy and the beauty of any of those things. We had so many conversations about all the good that came from him being here with us, but he couldn't see it. Now he was saying, "I can't do anything right. I can't even kill myself right."

I don't think I will ever forget those words that my dad uttered as he was lying in the hospital bed. I remember looking into his eyes and realizing that, besides disappointment and despair, there was so much shame and guilt. He didn't want to be around for tomorrow. But tomorrow needed him.

Tomorrow Needs You

This book is about growth after pain. Your trauma may be different from my trauma or my dad's trauma. Or you may not identify your past experiences as traumatic, but you still know they hurt. We all face negative experiences that can haunt us: lost relationships, disabilities, unemployment, difficult neighbors. Some of these experiences are intense and others are milder, but all of them have a cumulative effect on us. Regardless of your particular experience, this book is about being honest about our past fears and failures. It is about facing our trauma and our tragedies. It is about confronting our fears and our anxieties. It is about doing all of this not with more faith, but with beauty. In these pages, I will show you how it truly is the beautiful things in life that give us the power to overcome the most fearful things in life.

Moving On

It's said that knowledge can change us, but stories have the power to transform our lives. I believe this to be true. So, in this book, you will read stories in every chapter that illustrate the power of transformation. I have also taken the opportunity to share a lot of my childhood and my culture, hoping it will allow you to see that, regardless of a fearful past, God can create a beautiful future.

My prayer is that you will stop trying to find strength within yourself and instead look to what God is offering you. It starts with realizing that tomorrow needs you. Yes, it does. Your tomorrow and someone else's tomorrow need you. Although we spend so much time rehearsing the past, the reality is that yesterday has forgotten us, and today is waiting.

We Need to Be Needed

We all need to be needed. We are wired to be wanted. We need people. We begin to crack and eventually break when we feel unwanted or are convinced we are unnecessary. We all have days when we feel like nobody sees us, cares about us, understands us, or will miss us. We need God. We need counseling, therapy, walks, sleep, and so forth. We need whatever helps us to heal. Days like those are inevitable but also unreliable. We should not believe all those feelings. Those thoughts are connected to yesterday and a bad today, but tomorrow needs you. Tomorrow has so much potential, so much possibility. There are relationships and opportunities that need you. There are dreams that won't come true without you.

But life happens. We get sick. We lose jobs. We encounter tragedy, and everything changes. The life we knew becomes unfamiliar and unstable. We find ourselves struggling with disappointment and disillusionment. Most of the time our soul is trying to process what has happened to us, but our emotions have already started affecting our bodies. We begin to do things that we would never do. We begin to think thoughts that we would never have thought before. We end up not being able to see anything good in our lives. Pain and suffering create something so massive inside of us that at times the biggest giants we have to face are not in front of us but inside of us.

Do you find yourself not wanting to get out of bed? I know we have all felt this way. Maybe you're feeling it today, and you just don't think it's worth it. You had so much invested in yesterday. You had so many accomplishments and highs yesterday. But the past is too small for us to live in.

Forgetting the Past

In the Scriptures, the apostle Paul says, "I focus on this one thing: Forgetting the past and looking forward to what lies ahead, I press on to reach the end of the race and receive the heavenly prize for which God, through Christ Jesus, is calling us" (Philippians 3:13-14 NLT). Paul was talking to a certain group of people, but the content of his message rings true for us as well. We have to focus on tomorrow and not dwell on yesterday. I cannot help but wonder if he was reminded of the Old Testament passage in which God says, "Do not dwell on the past. See, I am doing a new thing! Now it springs up; do you not perceive it? I am making a way in the wilderness and streams in the wasteland" (Isaiah 43:18-19).

I wonder if sometimes we continue to worship the God of the past and don't recognize the God of the future. Because God exists in the future—he was in our yesterday, but he's also in tomorrow. It makes sense that God focuses on tomorrow and the future, because hope exists not in the past but only in the future. God is calling us, you and me; regardless of what happened to us, he's calling us to

Moving On

the future. He knows that our dreams and aspirations and all the beautiful things exist in the future. If we are consumed with the things of yesterday, we cannot tap into the possibility of tomorrow.

Maybe tomorrow is scary to you. Maybe because of what happened, you know for a fact that you could no longer be the person you were before. Your status has changed because now you are divorced. A loved one has died and now you are alone. You never thought you would be disabled, but even saying it now, knowing that you are, is so hard. And the thought of facing tomorrow with a permanent disability is terrifying. If tomorrow means that you have to trust again, love again, risk again, hope again, you don't want to face tomorrow.

In the book of Romans, Paul talks about pain, suffering, and God's love, and the connection between them. His writings in chapter 8 reveal that love is always questioned when pain and suffering are introduced in life. We question the love of the people in our lives when we are going through pain, grief, loss, or confusion. We question people's love when we go through relational conflict, difficulty at work, a chronic medical condition. We wonder, *Will she understand? Does he still like me? Are they still interested in me?* When we face failure and disappointment, we question people's commitment to us. We fear that if we continue to be unsuccessful and continue to struggle people will leave us. We question the love of everyone. We also question God's love when we go through tragedy and suffering. That is why Paul writes in Romans 8:38 (NLT): "I am convinced that nothing can ever separate us from God's love. Neither death nor life, neither angels nor demons, neither our fears for today nor our worries about tomorrow—not even the powers of hell can separate us from God's love." He wants to remind us, regardless of what we might feel, the truth that God has never left us.

14 PART ONE: YESTERDAY HAS FORGOTTEN YOU

So if you and I find ourselves in a place in which we have convinced ourselves that no one really cares, no one really notices, and no one really understands or loves us, then we are wrong. Our feelings are real and important, but they are not necessarily true. What is right and true? God's love and commitment toward us.

Yes, tomorrow can be scary. I think that is why King David (the one who was chosen, anointed, favored, and beloved by God, that guy), one of the most powerful men in history, struggled with fear and anxiety of tomorrow. The book of Psalms contains his confessions of weakness, doubt, and uncertainty. In Psalm 27, he unveils his practice of peace and power to face tomorrows: "The LORD is my light and my salvation—whom shall I fear? The LORD is the stronghold of my life—of whom shall I be afraid?" (Psalm 27:1).

Fears About Our Weaknesses

Tomorrow makes me nervous and anxious as well. Most people in my life would be surprised by that statement because I'm constantly talking about my new ideas of what the future could look like. There is no doubt that I love dreaming about the future, but that doesn't mean I don't have nightmares about it. I worry about whether people will find out that I'm not that smart, insightful, or interesting. So, yes, tomorrow might reveal to people that I'm not all that.

Tomorrow will test us. I have always hated taking tests. It started at an early age when I was in elementary school. You see, I have had a learning disability my whole life that made me a very bad test taker. Unfortunately, I did not find out I had a disability until I was in my forties. (I know, that's crazy, isn't it?) I believed for the longest time that I was simply not smart enough. To survive I started cheating on tests. I befriended the smart kids and convinced them to help me cheat. I did this from first to fifth grade. The older I got,

Moving On 15

the harder it got. Eventually, I developed stomachaches that would show up the nights before exams. I made myself sick so that I did not have to face tomorrow. Once it got so bad that the doctors thought I might have stomach worms.

All this because tomorrow was test day. That is the reason tomorrows are so hard for me. I'm tempted to live in today or dream about yesterday because a part of me feels like I will always do badly when tested. But if tomorrow is going to test me anyway in spite of my anxiety about it, then I choose to believe that tomorrow needs me. For everybody I love will be there tomorrow, and I need to be with them.

God's Call into Tomorrow

We also need words of truth as we move past our yesterday. In Jeremiah 1:5, God says to Jeremiah, "Before I formed you in the womb I knew you, before you were born I set you apart; I appointed you as a prophet to the nations."

It seems like God is saying, "Jeremiah, I have been dreaming about your future before you were born. I've got you, regardless of what you might think. You are special to me. I have uniquely created you for a purpose. This purpose is bigger than you think. I have known your yesterday. I'm in your today. And I'm calling you out to tomorrow."

Two

Learning to Trust

God Again

"Naeem, Ernest *chala gaya hai*."

My mom could barely talk, her voice cracking and trembling as she spoke. I could hear the horror in the silence and sense the weight of her soul in her words.

I have always been close to my sister Atiya. I grew up with two brothers and two sisters, but she is my favorite (don't tell the others). It has to be because of our mutual love of fashion or Bollywood—or both. Maybe it's because both of us have never met a mirror we didn't like. We developed a deeper connection as well when I prayed with her to start her relationship with Jesus. I will never forget that day. It was one of the most supernatural, unreal experiences of my life. Have you ever felt Jesus tangibly enter a room? We did that day!

Atiya came to the United States when she was seventeen. I can only imagine how hard that was for her, especially growing up as a conservative Muslim girl and being thrown into modern high

Learning to Trust God Again

school culture in the States. Of all my siblings, she most deeply loved her Pakistani culture, everything about it. So her hope was that she would marry a Pakistani. But what are the chances of that happening when most Pakistanis are Muslims? Loving the culture you were raised in while walking away from its faith makes it hard to find yourself. But then Atiya met Ernest, a Pakistani Christian, a rare breed. They started a beautiful friendship that led to marriage. International Family Church, led by Pastor Satish Raiborde, was their church. There they were a power couple leading various ministries, one of which was the youth ministry. They poured their lives into it. They loved those kids by creating a safe and nurturing space in their home. Ernest and Atiya loved them with their whole heart.

Then their daughter Jenna, was born—the joy of their life. Seven years later, Layla was born. Their joy was complete. Jenna was seven years old, and Layla was seven months old when it happened.

"Amiji, aap kya kah rahe hain?"

"Naeem, Ernest *mar gaya hai.*"

I could not believe what my mom was saying. Ernest had just died, and Atiya did not know. I did not want to believe my mom and asked her to explain. She said a neighbor who was a first responder was in the house, and so I asked to speak to him. He told me that Ernest had died of a heart attack. He told me that he tried his best to save him, but Ernest had already passed before the neighbor got there. I got off the phone with my mom and saw that my wife, Ashley, had sunk to the floor in horror because she overheard the conversation. We hugged briefly, and then I called my brother-in-law Paul and told him the news. I then grabbed my keys to get to Columbia, South Carolina, a two-hour drive away. I will never forget the scene when I arrived: The first responders were taking the body away. Atiya had waited for me to get there.

We hugged the entire time it took them to load Ernest's body in the vehicle and drive away.

"I can't do it," she said as her heart continued to break and tears streamed down her face. "I just can't do it. I can't tell Jenna that her dad has died. Could you please do it, Naeem?" Atiya pleaded with me.

Sometimes It's Hard to Trust God

It was January 15, 2018. My dad had just died January 23, 2017—a year before.

How do you tell a seven-year-old girl that her dad died today? You do it knowing that you will never be the same person again—that it will forever mark you.

Some todays can be traumatic. Days like those can leave you wondering if God exists and whether God cares. Subconsciously, we are convinced that todays are just opportunities for tragedies.

I love God, but sometimes I don't trust him.

Have you had that thought before? I do appreciate all that God does. I feel his grace and his acceptance of me. I understand his forgiveness, and I know that he loves me. But sometimes I don't trust him. I don't trust that he will keep me safe, that he will protect my family, that he will keep me from harm's way. I don't trust that he will let me know what's happening or be there when I need him the most.

There is a story in the Bible in which a man named Lazarus is sick. His sisters sent word to Jesus that if he doesn't show up soon Lazarus might die. Jesus waits for days before he heads to see Lazarus. On his way, he is confronted by one of the sisters.

"Lord," . . . "if you had been here, my brother would not have died." To which Jesus said, "I am the resurrection and the life. The one who believes in me will live, even though they die; and

Learning to Trust God Again

whoever lives by believing in me will never die. Do you believe this?" (John 11:21, 25-26).

This is one of those stories that reminds me that Jesus continues to make room for doubt in our lives. Doubt does not need to lead to a disbelief in God's ability, but rather it can lead to a deeper belief in God's character. So I embrace my doubt at these times knowing that God and I are about to get closer as we wrestle. Jesus in this story shows us that God doesn't remove doubt by answering all our questions but rather by drawing near to us. It's not the absence of uncertainty but rather the proximity of his presence that helps us in our doubt.

Our todays dare us to trust again.

From Coping to Creating

My coping mechanism is watching *The Office* and eating a particular kind of tortilla chips from Target. They are the yellow corn chips, not the blue or the white—the ones in the yellow bag. They are incredible. If you know, you know (IYKYK). One day my son said to me, "When you keep watching the same show and eating the same chips, you are managing anxiety."

My son is right. We can't keep coping; we have to start creating. Why do we keep watching the same shows on Netflix? There are so many shows on multiple streaming outlets. Could it be that there are too many options? Or is it that we are trying to escape reality for a minute? Do we desperately need relief from the weight of the life we are living? Disappointment, frustration, sadness, and worry each has a weight to it. And when it gets heavy we live our todays only to find relief. We distract ourselves with pleasure of any kind.

Today is waiting for you to show up. As Jesus said in John 9:4, the daylight is temporary; night is coming, and we have work to do today. What is keeping you from today? Are you running out the clock by wasting time, or are you making the time to do what needs to be done today? The Scriptures tell us in Lamentations 3:23 that God's blessings are new every day. So your every day has the potential to be a new today. Regardless of our failures or losses, we can gain ground today.

Posttraumatic Growth

It has been very challenging to have a Middle Eastern background and start a church in the South. I've heard a lot of outrageous opinions and been called some pretty off-the-wall things, but I never realized how hard it would be for people to attend a church led by a Pakistani, former Muslim man. An example of the kinds of conversations I have is the time that I reached out to a volunteer and said: "Hey, I've noticed you've been volunteering for a while. I really do appreciate that you're out here in the foyer helping people with coffee, but I don't think I've ever seen you in the auditorium."

I didn't mean to be this forward, but he had been attending Mosaic, the church I lead, for a while now. The man said: "Yeah, actually I tried to go into the auditorium a couple of times but I just can't do it. It's just that I served in the Afghanistan war, and people who looked like you were the enemy. I've had some near-death experiences of being peppered with gunfire by people who look like you. So don't take it the wrong way, I just can't be in an enclosed space with you."

Wow! I had never heard that before! The man in the lobby admittedly suffered from posttraumatic stress disorder (PTSD). According to the Substance Abuse and Mental Health Services Administration (SAMHSA), PTSD

Learning to Trust God Again 21

develops when a person has experienced or witnessed a scary, shocking, terrifying, or dangerous event. These stressful or traumatic events usually involve a situation in which some-one's life has been threatened or severe injury has occurred. . . . You can get PTSD after living through or seeing a traumatic event, such as war, a natural disaster, sexual assault, physical abuse, or a bad accident. PTSD makes you feel stressed and afraid after the danger is over. It affects your life and the people around you.

PTSD starts at different times for different people. Signs of PTSD may start soon after a frightening event and then continue. Other people develop new or more severe signs months or even years later.

You might be very familiar with PTSD. Either you struggle with it or have loved ones that do. But have you heard of posttraumatic growth (PTG)?

Aamer is the only Pakistani-Korean guy I know. He might be the only one in the world. He is a fellow CrossFitter and is married to the spunkiest Palestinian lady I know, Shadia. By the time this book comes out, they will have had beautiful twin boys. One day after a workout, Aamer and I began talking about PTG.

"Yeah, I thought I would be in the military for life," Aamer said. But that thought changed one day when, while his unit was clearing a town, a bomb blew off. He almost broke his neck and died.

According to the Department of Psychological Science, Post-traumatic Growth Research Group at the University of North Carolina at Charlotte, PTG is the "positive change experienced as a result of the struggle with a major life crisis or a traumatic event." The Boulder Crest Foundation explains that the idea that human beings can be changed by their encounters with life challenges, sometimes in radically positive ways, is not new. The theme is present in ancient spiritual and religious traditions, literature, and philosophy. What is reasonably new is the systematic study of this phenomenon by psychologists, social workers, counselors, and scholars in other traditions of clinical practice and scientific investigation. The Boulder Crest Foundation identifies five domains of posttraumatic growth:

1. New possibilities: opening ourselves to previously intangible opportunities.
2. Deeper relationships: discovering richer connections when we share our suffering with others.
3. Personal strength: growing in the belief that "if I can get through this, I can get through anything."
4. Appreciation for life: cultivating gratitude for what we have and recognizing what matters most to us.
5. Spiritual and existential change: learning to ask deeper questions about the meaning of life.

Maybe you've experienced this posttraumatic growth yourself. You've gone through a traumatic childhood, and now you're more resilient as an adult. You've gone through a life-altering event, but you came out of it more confident. You've been a victim of hate and prejudice, but that has made you kinder and more compassionate. You've experienced spiritual abuse for most of your life, yet you find yourself passionately following Jesus. You've lived in extreme poverty, yet you are extravagantly generous with your possessions and resources.

But how do we grow? We grow by facing fears.

Learning to Trust God Again 23

How Do We Begin to Face Our Fears?

I had an early experience with needles that created a longtime fear in me. My mom is a seamstress, and she has been her whole life. She loves that I love fashion. I have childhood memories of designing clothing with her. During one of those great moments, I remember she asked me to come sit down with her, and I sat down on a needle. Wow! I don't think I'll ever forget that moment—ever! Imagine the privilege of pulling a needle out of your butt cheek.

Every time I'm around her now I clear the seat before I sit down Needless to say, I'm not a fan of needles. So when my physical therapist suggested that he was going to needle my calf and hamstrings and then connect electrical charges to them, I was a little bit apprehensive. Since I knew him, I was like, "Bro, do we really need to do this?" In the end I did give him permission to do that, and I'm grateful I did. I learned that needles are not always to be feared—they can also help in healing.

Jesus, when he walked among us, was always concerned with the holistic healing of an individual. In fact, the word *sōzō*, when used in the New Testament, is translated variously as "save, heal, make whole, deliver." The first use of the word is in Matthew 1:21 in which the Lord speaks to Joseph in a dream to tell him not to be afraid of taking Mary as his wife. The Lord says, "She will give birth to a son, and you are to give him the name Jesus [which means "Savior"], because he will save [Greek, *sōzō*] his people from their sins." Saving from sin is an important work of Jesus on the cross as it brings us into relationship with the Father, but salvation doesn't end there. Jesus was concerned about every aspect of our lives, including our physical, emotional, and psychological well-being.

As we face our internal and external fears, the good news is that God has also given us direct access to his Spirit, who speaks to us.

24 PART ONE: YESTERDAY HAS FORGOTTEN YOU

His Word, as the book of Hebrews says, "is alive and powerful. It is sharper than the sharpest two-edged sword, cutting between soul and spirit, between joint and marrow. It exposes our innermost thoughts and desires" (Hebrews 4:12 NLT).

That is why moving from yesterday into today starts with facing God with our fears. We can do this because of who Jesus is and what he has done for us. Later, in the same letter to the Hebrews, it reminds the people: "For we do not have a high priest who is unable to empathize with our weaknesses, but we have one who has been tempted in every way, just as we are—yet he did not sin. Let us then approach God's throne of grace with confidence, so that we may receive mercy and find grace to help us in our time of need" (Hebrews 4:15-16).

God wants to go into today with you. But it is a choice.

My sister Atiya has to decide every day whether to walk into today or live in yesterday. Because yesterday she lost her husband and all they had built together. Every today she faces her fears and reminds herself that God is faithful. God knows that it's so hard for some of us to face today. We are filled with anxiety and doubt; we are preoccupied with negative thoughts and consumed with confusion. God knows us fully. That is why he's able to love us completely. God is not waiting around for you to get it together and to feel great. God is extending his hand to you, wanting you to grab hold of it. He knows if we do it together with him we can face our most fearful today.

Part Two

Today Is Waiting

A blurry tomorrow still needs you to see clearly today.

No one likes to wait. And we all have different responses to waiting, depending on what or who we are waiting on. Momentary waiting can build excitement and energy, but ceaseless waiting erodes our joy and makes us weary. What if your body was waiting on your soul? What if God's Spirit was waiting on your soul—waiting for you to act, to take the next best step? What if your friends and family were waiting on you?

We can feel paralyzed in our todays, waking up and not wanting to face the day. Our worries can make us weary. But we can't allow fear of yesterday's loss, pain, and regret to hold us down.

The Scriptures tell us God's perfect love has the power to cast out our fear, and he extends his hand to us today. "I believe; help my unbelief!" This plea to Jesus in Mark 9:24 reminds me that it is okay to move with doubt and fear as long as we move. Because when we do, God is with us every step of the way.

So, let's allow to God to lead us; let's trust him as much as we can and stop making today wait on us.

Three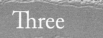

My Relationship

with Fear

"I'm going to kill you. You're going to die," it said to me as it came closer and closer.

I'm not quite sure how I understood what this thing was saying, but I believed it. I was physically paralyzed in that moment, not by my fear but by some invisible forces that I could not really understand. Demons. That's what came to mind. One had pinned me to my bed, disabled me to the point that I only had control of my neck. At first I thought it was a dream, but I had not even gone to bed. As one tightened its grip, another enormous demon got closer and closer.

I had been in the States for only three weeks. My dad had figured out a way to get me a tourist visa to see my brother Mahmood in Charleston, South Carolina. Our hope was that I would somehow find a way to get into college, having left the war-torn country of Kuwait. "Don't come back, Naeem. There's nothing here for you," my dad said to me at the airport when I left for the States. The moment was filled with excitement and an underlying fear of uncertainty. I had no idea the kind of fears I would be facing when I got to the States.

I knew Mahmood was no longer Muslim. Several years prior, he told my siblings and me that he was a follower of Christ, was born again, and was no longer following Islam. I did not agree with his choices at that time. Mahmood also mentioned he was going to let Mom and Dad know, but I convinced him to keep his mouth shut.

Those three weeks went by so fast. They were full of new experiences, one of which was going to weekly collegiate Fellowship of Christian Athletes meetings where I first heard the message of Jesus. I'd never heard that there was ever a possibility of having an intimate, meaningful, and unique relationship with God. My brother was convinced that Jesus would reveal himself to me if I asked him to—which made me think that my brother should be medicated. But his confidence was so intriguing.

One night I asked Jesus if he would reveal himself to me. Three days after that, I found myself face to face with a demon. I can't explain or describe that moment. It was so big that it didn't even feel real, even though I was experiencing real terror, horror, dread, and fear. It was too much. In fact, I thought it was a different dimension that I found myself in.

As soon as the demon reached my bed, it disappeared. Whatever was holding me let go, and I found myself stunned, lying in my bed. I slowly sat up, and then I ran as fast as I could to wake up my brother to tell him what happened. In my book *Ex-Muslim*, I go into more detail; but long story short, I went back into the same room and met Jesus. Yes, he showed up. I can't explain what I saw as I looked at him. His presence was peace illuminated. "Your life is not your own," he said. Those words directed my purpose. Those words have anchored my soul. Those words have dismantled fear in my life.

How Childhood Fears Shape Us

I distinctly remember the day I was first aware of feeling fear. I know it sounds strange and even funny to say, but it was the day I watched the original *Planet of the Apes* movie. The characters frightened me so much that I slept with my mom and dad for a week. I also faintly remember watching Alfred Hitchcock movies and realizing that some of them didn't just spook me but would terrorize me at night. I quickly became afraid of the dark. I must admit that I still get spooked at night.

Growing up, I feared not only monsters but also math! I had multiple fears of inadequacy when it came to academics. And I dreaded test taking. Learning was hard for me. I did not realize until later in my forties that I have a learning disability. Come to find out, I have dyslexia and dysgraphia. Both are neurological conditions that can be related. With dyslexia, a person has difficulty with spelling, reading, and writing. With dysgraphia, the person has difficulty writing. So as a kid and young adult I feared reading aloud, spelling words, and so forth.

I was also fearful about not fitting in. It did not help that I wasn't really good at cricket or soccer; I liked art.

Do you know your deepest fears? What do you do with them? How do you dismantle them? Can you conquer them? I know you can. I know this because I've had to fight so many battles with fear in my life.

Fighting Our Demons

Maybe you did not grow up in a faith that talked about supernatural things. For me, as Muslim, we really did not talk about these things, either, so I had an ignorant view of them. I believed they were possibly true, but I had no concrete belief until I was faced with this clear and present danger in my life—a very good reason to fear! That night, when I was introduced to the unseen world, I had to face the reality that life is no fairytale. It is filled with fearful things.

Fear did not stop that night. In one sense, it opened up more scary doors that I knew I had to walk through. I remember my reaction when my brother turned his back on Islam. Islam is more than a global religion; in a sense it's a global nationality, one founded on the belief that there is one God and one prophet. To be born into and raised in that faith and then reject it was to reject Allah and his prophet. And there were consequences for that. Based on traditional Sharia law, it was punishable by death. Some Muslim countries still practice that law. That is the basis of how I eventually got religious asylum and was living as a refugee in the States.

When I became a Christian, I felt intense joy in the love of Jesus but also fear as I prepared to share my experience with my family. I could not imagine how my siblings and my parents would feel when I told them that I was no longer a Muslim. Now I was the apostate, the defector, the traitor of the faith.

My first month as a follower of Jesus was filled with immense amounts of uncertainty, fear, anxiety, and supernatural peace, hope, and love. I wish I could say that meeting Jesus dismantled the fear in my life, but that's simply not true. And it's not how he works. God still wants us to be strong and courageous as we face the uncertainty of our lives. There was so much uncertainty in my life during my first year in the United States. I had no idea how things would pan out, how I would get to stay in the country, how my parents would react to my conversion, and if people would even believe my incredibly ridiculous story.

My Relationship with Fear

How Fear Affects Our Brains and Our Bodies

Fear is a normal biological condition that all humans experience. It can have positive and negative consequences. Fear has the ability to heighten our awareness of self. Fear is programmed into the nervous system and works like an instinct. We are equipped with the survival instincts necessary to respond with fear when we sense danger or feel unsafe. Fear helps protect us. It makes us alert to danger and prepares us to deal with it.

According to Dr. Zachary Sikora, at Northwestern Medicine,

as soon as you recognize fear, your amygdala (small organ in the middle of your brain) goes to work. It alerts your nervous system, which sets your body's fear response into motion. Stress hormones like cortisol and adrenaline are released. Your blood pressure and heart rate increase. You start breathing faster. Even your blood flow changes—blood actually flows away from your heart and into your limbs, making it easier for you to start throwing punches, or run for your life.

But did you know that fear can make you foggy or even freaky? While fear activates certain parts of the brain, it causes other parts to go into shut-down mode. The cerebral cortex is the area of the brain that oversees our ability to reason and make judgments. It becomes debilitated in fearful situations, making it difficult to think clearly and rationally. For some people, however, the experience of fear can be pleasurable. Do you love roller coasters, haunted houses, scary movies, or anything that scares the junk out of you? No shade here; maybe I'm just not brave enough. But I do understand why you do. As Dr. Sikora says, "During a staged fear experience, your brain will produce more of a chemical called dopamine, which elicits pleasure."

Fear is a normal response to events or objects. Phobias, on the other hand, are a more extreme form of fear that get in the way of normal functioning and everyday activities. If you start taking drastic measures to avoid certain things, situations, or people, you may have a phobia. That could look like refusing to drive, like my dad after he had a heart attack while driving, or people refusing to ride an elevator because it's too confined of a place. During the global Covid-19 pandemic, many people displayed agoraphobic behaviors that affected their social development and quality of life. Do you think you have a phobia of the future that has paralyzed you in the present?

Fear isolates you. Some of us know exactly what that means because we've allowed fear to not only paralyze us but also isolate us from so many people in our lives. One friend put it this way: "I don't go out much anymore, and I'm an extrovert," he confessed. When we are crippled with fear or anxiety that has turned into depression, we want to be alone. We are embarrassed of our feelings. We can't explain to someone else what we can't even put into words ourselves. I can't help but recall the lyrics of the song "The Sound of Silence," by Simon and Garfunkel: "Hello darkness, my old friend. I've come to talk with you again."

How Fear Lies to Us

Fear comes in like a roommate and does not leave. Fear is a squatter. Fear is no friend, and it's even worse as an enemy. As soon as we don't give it as much attention as it needs, it turns on us. It reminds us of our shame, guilt, regret, and possible failure. It brings out the worst. Its goal is to stop us, to paralyze us, to hold us hostage. It wants to expel courage from us. Don't get me wrong, it's a smooth talker, and at times I have gotten tricked by all that it says. Fear

My Relationship with Fear   33

makes a great argument for why we should not attempt things, why we should never try to step out or take chances. It reminds us what will happen when we fail, and what people will think about us. It wants to save us from embarrassment. It's concerned about our image.

Fear promises us self-preservation, but it does not tell us it will cause us to self-decay. Fear tells us that it will keep us safe. If we only listen to fear, we will not have to face rejection, loss, betrayal, or trauma. Fear tells us that there is a world out there that wants to hurt us, so the best thing to do is to stay cooped up in this room. But what fear does not tell us is that this room is a prison. It's comfortable, but it's a cage. Fear does not want us to have freedom. But we were never meant to be confined or caged by anything. "It is for freedom that Christ has set us free" (Galatians 5:1). It is only with freedom that we are formed into people of destiny. Captivity conforms us to mediocrity.

Fear leaves out the part about how our spirit, soul, and body will begin to atrophy if we choose to not step out of fear. We as human beings were created to move toward everything that God has for us. Genesis 1:26 (NLT) records God saying, "Let us make human beings in our image, to be like us." The "us" in this passage reveals that God is Trinity. The word "Trinity" comes from the Latin word *trinus,* which means "threefold"—God the Father, the Son, and the Holy Spirit. God has made us in his image.

Fear wants to control us. The only way to conquer fear is to dismantle it, facing what we are most afraid of right now in our lives. For me, early in my faith, I found solace in Psalm 27. I feel at times that it was written solely for me. More than reading it, I love declaring it: "The LORD is my light and my salvation—whom shall I fear? The LORD is the stronghold of my life—of whom shall I be afraid?" There are so many times I have had to say it out loud so that my soul, spirit, and body can hear and absorb it. These are words of resolve and intention. The resolve is that I will not let fear be the stronghold of my life, and the intention is that I will move forward toward light and salvation, toward my hopes and dreams.

What about you? What are you afraid of? The basic trigger for fear is the threat of harm, whether real or imagined. This threat can be for our physical, emotional, or spiritual well-being. While there are certain things that trigger fear in most of us, we can learn to become afraid of nearly anything if we let fear lead us.

Are you afraid you will never be successful, never be married, never have financial security, never truly be free of addiction? Has fear promised you protection and security while all along locking you in a room? It's a mediocre room, but it's pleasant enough to keep you unaware that it's actually a prison. I have lived there. It's comfortable until it's not. But by then it's too late; opportunities have passed by, and relationships that could have been significant are no longer an option.

It reminds me of the bomb shelters we rushed to during the Gulf War. There were many nights when we were awakened and taken to the shelters to keep us safe from possible bombs. Even though these were safe places and we were secure and safe momentarily, retreating to these places did not help create momentum in our lives. We were just stuck there—safe, but not really going anywhere in life.

We all have our own battles to fight, our own wars that we have to face. Sometimes we've had great victories, but at other times we have suffered much loss and trauma. We can't keep running and trying to live in bomb shelters because we are afraid of what could happen. There are no victories won in bomb shelters. We have to choose whether security or purpose is the goal in our lives. We can't have both. Don't get me wrong; we need to feel a sense of security. God promises to provide that, but it's usually in the middle of a battlefield.

God and Fear

"*Khuda ka khauf karo*, Naeem." I heard this statement all the time when I was growing up. My Pakistani mom would say this Urdu phrase to motivate me to get in line. It means "fear God." There was this sense of doing the right thing because God was watching, and he was a punisher of people doing the wrong thing. My mom would use this line all the time; the fear of God was a constant form of behavior modification used on me. I'm not quite sure if she knew what she was doing, but fear and God were always linked together in the negative. We can become conditioned to feel certain feelings deeply when key words are associated with trauma or experiences that were negative. As a result of this, whenever I thought of God, it was in anticipation of judgment and punishment.

Despite the fact that we may know better, followers of Jesus can fall into the trap of using fear as a motivator to do things for God. But then we realize fear is not a friend; it's an enemy. There is a holy reverence of the majesty of God, who is the Creator of all the universe, and there is a sense of awe and wonder when we think about how expansive he is. But, unfortunately, the word *fear* does not convey the sense that God wants us to have when we think of him. For some of us, our spirituality is connected to fear. We did things and did not do things because we feared God. Some of us were told we would go to hell if we were to do certain things, and the fear of a loss of salvation motivated us to do good. Such tactics are actually manipulation. Unfortunately, when you use fear, fear begins to use you. When you use fear to control people, fear begins to control you. If you are a Lord of the Rings fan, you understand the ring of power. Yes, it gives you the ability to do some incredible things, but it changes you incredibly.

We have to put a leash on fear, or it will put a leash on us.

Currently, I have two cats—not because I love cats, but because I love my wife and daughter. However, I would prefer a dog—in fact, a Doberman. For years I have seen people walk their dogs and I've always wondered who is really in charge. But as long as the leash is on the animal and not the owner, we can be hopeful that the owner is in charge.

Fear serves a purpose in our lives—but only if we are able to keep it leashed. It takes intention to use fear to our benefit. As kids, we learn to pay attention to our fears because they help us to navigate danger. Learning to recognize and process our fear responses is a part of healthy human development. But it's tricky because fear can be a master manipulator. Fear wants to cuddle up beside you and promise you all kinds of loyalty, while subversively dismantling and paralyzing your hopes and dreams. That is why we have to put a leash on our fears before they put a leash on us.

In the next several chapters we will talk about different kinds of fears. My hope is that we will identify them so that we can tame them. We cannot allow fear to tell us that yesterday still remembers us, today can wait for us, and no one truly needs us tomorrow. As God told Jeremiah, "Before I formed you in the womb I knew you, before you were born I set you apart" (Jeremiah 1:5). We can speak to our fear because God is with us today.

Four

Fear of Loss

People ask me all the time what it was like to go through a war. It was surreal, and there were moments in the war that I did not know if we would ever make it out. By the end of the war, we were running out of food and water. Electricity was in short supply and so was hope. In war, everybody loses; there are no winners. Although one side might declare victory, people on both sides lose precious things.

I lost friendships in the war. Some of them I lost the day the war broke out, because of lack of communication or because they fled the country. After all these years, I still don't know what became of them. It's strange how one day we're laughing and playing together, and the next day we never see each other. There were no goodbyes; there were no farewells.

Sometimes loss comes out of nowhere and sideswipes us, causing us to spin around in surprise, dread, and uncertainty. There are other times when loss slowly eats away precious time. That was the case when I was stuck in the war, realizing that most of my teenage years were going to be given over to a conflict that I was not a part of. I was simply one of the civilian casualties of decisions that people in power made.

As I process the fear of loss in my own life, I find that I'm okay with losing if I know there is a reason. But if there is no reason for the loss, I either continue on and on trying to figure it out, or I drown myself in grief.

I sometimes find myself thinking about all the relationships and friendships that I lost during the Covid-19 pandemic. But it was not just Covid; it was also the political climate at the time. Some of the relationships I honestly haven't even come to terms with because I don't want to feel the loss.

I recall my feelings when Arvind yelled at me: "I hate that you became a Christian! How could you?! What is wrong with you?" We didn't talk for years after that.

I can't believe it's happening. I never thought it would come to this. Is this really happening? Those were my thoughts as I was trying to figure out what went wrong and why I was losing this friendship that was decades old. *Why is it ending so poorly?* I thought. *Why is it happening now? What did I do wrong? Maybe I should've been more attentive. Maybe I should've focused more on the relationship. Is this going to be forever? Am I going to lose him forever?* I'm so thankful that it wasn't *forever.* Arvind and I were able to reconcile and are still best of friends to this day. But some of my friendships weren't that fortunate.

I Don't Like Losing

We don't like losing things that are precious to us. These things can be relationships, careers, friendship, success, or security. Regardless of what it is, if it's important, the loss is felt deeply, uniquely, and profoundly. In fact, these kinds of losses can leave deep wounds and permanent scars on our souls.

Have you been wounded or scarred by loss in your life and now find yourself developing fear of losing things that are precious to

Fear of Loss 39

you? We have to look at the kinds of fears we struggle with the most. For some of us, it is the fear of loss. *Fear* and *loss*—these two words don't work for me. As you already know, I've got this issue with fear, like we all do. Mine is that I don't like losing! I like keeping my relationships and my friendships. I like keeping the level of my success and the security that comes with that.

What do you fear losing? What's most important to you right now?

Some of us have lost in love. Although we know that Shakespeare says it is better to have loved and lost than to have never loved at all, we may be tempted to think that Shakespeare had no clue about what he was talking about. For if he had felt the loss we have felt, he would have written that it is definitely better to have never loved at all. I know this isn't necessarily true, but this is how we can feel, and it's okay to feel this way. It's okay to feel the fear of loss.

Looking for My People

It's not just individuals who break our hearts. Dread comes when you know you might lose a friend group. I have always wanted to have a "tribe." I don't mean the ancient tribal culture. I'm talking about this idea of "my people." But I've always struggled with finding a tribe. It seems like I never quite fit in.

In reality, I've always been an immigrant. I was born in Kuwait, if you remember, but my parents are Pakistani. So I lived in a foreign country most of my life—always as a foreigner. I wasn't Kuwaiti; I was a Pakistani. But I never lived in Pakistan. I was not raised there. Even when we would visit Pakistan, my cousins would pick on me about how I was really not a true Pakistani. I didn't talk or act like one. I knew the language, but acting like a Pakistani, I didn't really get.

If you have ever been an immigrant or a foreigner in a country, you know that we begin to take on the characteristics of the dominant culture in which we live. So I acted like a Kuwaiti, maybe? Regardless, I did not fit within "my people." Then I came to the United States, to Charleston, South Carolina, and I did not fit in at all. I didn't look, talk, or act like a southerner. "You ain't from around here" is a phrase I would soon get used to.

This notion of not fitting continued when I became a Christian. I didn't fit a certain denomination. I obviously didn't fit the mold of how you're supposed to come to faith in Jesus. I didn't "come to the altar," if you know what I mean.

What's really confusing to an eighteen-year-old kid is when well-meaning Christians realize there's a sense of purpose on you. They automatically think that your purpose is to go back and reach "your people." Little did they know, I didn't have a group called "my people." But by assuming that I did, and that "my people" were back in the Middle East, those well-meaning Christians were inadvertently letting me know that they were not "my people" either.

Starting Mosaic Church has been beautiful in so many ways, but it has come with the loss of so many relationships. Even though this is a natural part of church work, I never anticipated that. And I never realized that I had the loudest laughs with people who would make me cry the hardest.

It's not just the loss of people or my teenage years but also the loss of success and momentum that bothers me. I think for so many of us there is a serious fear of losing success, the connections we have made, and the status we've been able to reach. We're fearful of the loss of resources and money. We're fearful of the loss of security in our lives because of the jobs that we have; we fear losing

Fear of Loss 41

them. We have worked so hard to save for the future and we fear the loss of it.

Losing people, opportunities, or momentum can leave a scar. And the memory of that pain keeps us from our potential. *I'm just waiting for the next terrible thing to happen.* Have you ever had that thought? When you've worked so hard to create a certain kind of life or have put in so much work to build something, it is so traumatic to lose it. The grief that comes with loss is unique to the person and what was lost. No one goes through grief well. No one enjoys loss.

Everything That Has Happened Will Be Redeemed

So where is God when you lose someone or something precious to you?

It's okay to ask why. *Why, God, did you let this happen? Why would you not tell me? Why didn't you stop me?* These are all great questions. Sometimes we in the Christian faith are told to ask not why but what. I understand the thought behind that. Within the *religion* of Christianity we are not to question, but in a *relationship* with Jesus, we get to ask. *Why did you not show up? If you would have only showed up, this would not be happening to me.* I, for one, encourage you to ask and wrestle with God about the why. Why? Because Jesus tells us that God is inviting us into a friendship, not another faith. And in this relationship with God, like any relationship, we get to ask why. Our relationship with Christ gets reduced to religion when we start asking only transactional questions like *What do I need to do, God, so that you will do your part?* Jesus wants us to ask the harder questions of him and share our deepest disappointment with him.

In John 11:21 (NLT), Martha said to Jesus, "Lord, if only you had been here, my brother would not have died." Can you feel the

42 PART TWO: TODAY IS WAITING

distress and disappointment in her voice? I can imagine that interaction as she confronts Jesus about why he didn't show up when her brother was dying, even though Jesus knew days before that Lazarus was deathly ill. Why did God allow the illness to get this bad and for Lazarus to lose his life?

I'm convinced that at times God allows—and maybe even creates—opportunities in which we can struggle with serious doubt. Because with Jesus doubt does not need to lead to disbelief but rather a deeper sense of belief. Martha, in her next statement, alludes to this: "But even now I know that God will give you whatever you ask" (Luke 11:22 NLT).

Have you ever heard the pithy expression "Everything happens for a reason"? I truly dislike that expression. It seems like there is an element of hope in it. But this kind of hope is a false hope that opens us up for disappointment. Proverbs 13:12 (NLT) says that "hope deferred makes the heart sick." A hope deferred is a hope that believes that things will surely turn around soon. The key word is *soon*. And when soon doesn't happen soon enough our faith begins to fade.

"Everything that has happened will be redeemed" is my expression when I see tragic, horrific loss. I find solace in Revelation 21:4 (NLT), which says that one day God "will wipe every tear from their eyes, and there will be no more death or sorrow or crying or pain. All these things are gone forever." Forgive me if I seem flippant, but if you have lost things so precious and you fear losing more things in the future, God will redeem. The loss does have a purpose, but we might not see it on this side of heaven.

Helen Keller said, "No pessimist ever discovered the secrets of the stars, or sailed to an uncharted land, or opened a new heaven to the human spirit.... Optimism is the faith that leads to

Fear of Loss 43

achievement." I fully believe this, but it's a resilient optimism that makes the difference. Whereas hope is based on things working out or situations changing for our good, this resilient optimism is anchored in God, who holds all things. God is our only true hope.

The Gospel of John records Jesus explaining that sometimes God causes necessary endings to certain relationships, opportunities, and seasons for a bigger purpose. Jesus says,

> I am the true grapevine, and my Father is the gardener. He cuts off every branch of mine that doesn't produce fruit, and he prunes the branches that do bear fruit so they will produce even more. You have already been pruned and purified by the message I have given you. Remain in me, and I will remain in you. For a branch cannot produce fruit if it is severed from the vine, and you cannot be fruitful unless you remain in me.
>
> Yes, I am the vine; you are the branches. Those who remain in me, and I in them, will produce much fruit. For apart from me you can do nothing. (John 15:1-5 NLT)

Jesus is talking about things that will matter for eternity, that will shape our character and our quality of life. Those things require us to stay close to God's presence to possess his promises. God prunes us, and often that looks like loss. But he does it to make us even more fruitful, to remind us that God understands how losing a part of who we are is painful. It can seem like God is upset with us and punishing us, but he is not. It's not that God is repaying us for our sins. Instead, he knows that losing this one relationship or season is essential for our growth. Again I say, as much as this is true, it doesn't feel good most of the time. God knows this. That's why Jesus talks about it. He understands that we don't do well with loss, and that if we can't see where he is in the middle of it, we can begin to have a fear of loss.

That is why I have to remind myself, and I want to remind you, that the fear of losing everything will keep us from gaining everything God has for us.

J. R. R. Tolkien writes:

All that is gold does not glitter
Not all those who wander are lost;
The old that is strong does not wither,
Deep roots are not reached by the frost.

You might not be a Lord of the Rings fan, but there's so much truth in this quote. One of those truths is that God can do a deeper work in us and for us. Though it might not "glitter" or look good, it produces a rich life. I think of my now richer friendships because of the loss of other ones.

Also, when I find myself witnessing a "wandering" of relationships, there is still hope that they're not lost. If you are being tormented by the idea of losing your kids, your marriage, your family and friends, and your security and success, just know that they are not truly lost. They might just be wandering. Personally, I have had to remind myself of this in some rough seasons with my kids. I have to remember that I sowed good seeds and have nurtured deep roots. So although they seem to wander, they are not lost. And with God, everything is redeemable.

It is this hope of a future redemption that conquers the fear of loss in your life.

Five

Fear of Failure

"You will always be a failure." I will never forget those words.

I had walked into the fifth grade classroom on the first day of school (a little late because I did not want to be there at all), and the teacher asked, "Are you supposed to be in this class?" She was convinced that it wasn't right. I remember wondering, *Are you saying this because I'm taller than you and all the kids in the class?* Yes, it was the right class, but the problem was me. The teacher asked me to go to the principal's office with her, and now I was outside waiting while she talked with the principal.

What is wrong with you, Naeem? I thought. *Why are you even in school? The world doesn't need you. You are so dumb!* The voices were loud. I was embarrassed to be alive.

My teacher walked out of the office and said, "He wants to see you." *Why?* I thought. *I don't want to do this. I can't do this.* She reached for my hand, but I didn't want to take hers. I wanted to tell her that I'm not worth it. Did she know that I had failed fifth grade, repeated it, and failed again? The only reason I was in this Pakistani school was because the Indian school kicked me out. Did she realize that I had also failed the entrance exam to get into sixth grade?

But her hand was still extended, waiting for me to take it. I did.

PART TWO: TODAY IS WAITING

We walked into the principal's office together. She stepped to the corner of the office and left me standing alone in front of him. This principal looked like a judge who was going to sentence me. My fate rested on him. He looked up from his desk, glanced at the teacher, and started talking. I don't think I will ever forget his words:

"Your teacher here thinks that you are too old to be in her class. You have repeated fifth grade twice and, because of that, were expelled from your previous school. And now you are here in my school. You have failed the placement test to be enrolled into sixth grade. But for some reason she thinks, if she works with you, in two weeks you will be able to pass the placement to be in the sixth grade. What do you think?"

I could barely lift my eyes to look at him. "I think I can," I said, my lips not wanting to open to say anything else.

"Let me tell you what I think," he said. "I know kids like you. You are a failure, and you will always be a failure."

All that I can recall from that moment is feeling crushing humiliation and a deep rage. The next thing I remember was that I was in the hallway with the math teacher. She pulled my face close to hers and, looking straight into my soul, said, "Don't believe anything he said. I know you can do this. We are going to do this!"

Thirty-eight years later, I still tear up recalling this memory. Writing it down is painful.

Learning to Pretend

Why did the principal say those words to me? I think I know why. I grew up in an honor culture in which people believe that protecting and defending one's reputation and social image is most important. This culture believes that shame motivates. In the principal's case, I'm not quite sure if he was trying to motivate me or

Fear of Failure 47

protect his own reputation. But neither one of them worked. Honor culture perpetuates shaming behavior. This might be why I struggle with my image, always wanting to come across as put-together and successful. I thought the next best thing to being successful was to come across as if I were. So since I knew I wasn't smart, I just had to figure out a way to pretend that I was. I'm not sure when I gave up trying in school. I only remember finding it impossible to learn. It seemed that I wasn't good in any subject. The only way I could pass my classes was to cheat on every test. So I went to work at six or seven years old, making friends with all the smart students.

My plan worked until it didn't. Once I could not cheat my way through tests, I started failing classes and was faced with the thought that I was simply not smart enough for school. These failures informed my identity, telling me I was not enough in a lot ways.

We all have a relationship with fear, and a particularly unique one with the fear of failure. This relationship depends on past experiences with failure. It can inform our identity and our security. For me, it created a fear of not being smart enough, capable enough, or talented enough. This relationship becomes a vicious cycle of believing that we are not enough for others or ourselves, that we are not enough for others to like us, respect us, be attracted to us, or love us. When we internalize this, we convince ourselves that we shouldn't be satisfied with who we are. In a strange way, we become the judge, jury, and plaintiff, sentencing ourselves to a life of fear.

This persistent fear turns into anxiety pretty quickly. Anxiety begins to shape our lives, creating unhealthy habits, informing our decision-making, choosing our friendships, and navigating our intimate relationships. Renowned psychologist Dr. Paul Ekman says that this kind of anxiety "can be considered a disorder when it is

48   PART TWO: TODAY IS WAITING

recurrent, persistent, intense, and interferes with basic life tasks such as work and sleep."

It's interesting that we use the word *disorder* to describe some of our conditions because the word is the best way to see how fear and anxiety can order our steps. Fear of failure can disorder our lives and illuminate a path that leads to darkness. It's not a darkness that's necessarily evil; it just makes us comfortable living our lives closed off, always protecting ourselves. This darkness invites us to live in the shadows. This darkness promises us peace and protection that is just propaganda. It shows up in different ways in all of our relationships. It begins to develop into a fear of failing people, but then it does something even worse. It makes us hold other people to a standard that we ourselves are pretending to keep. All this pretending makes us more and more comfortable with darkness and uncomfortable with light. We become people who are not authentic or open. We become people who are extremely uncomfortable with vulnerability and weakness. We become people we were never created to be.

God loves us purely for who we are. And we are not made to live in darkness. King David was convinced of this as well. He writes:

If I try to hide in the darkness, the night becomes light around me. For even darkness cannot hide from God; to you the night shines as bright as day. Darkness and light are both alike to you.

You made all the delicate, inner parts of my body and knit them together in my mother's womb. Thank you for making me so wonderfully complex! It is amazing to think about. Your workmanship is marvelous—and how well I know it. (Psalm 139:11-14 TLB)

Fear of Failure   49

This is a beautiful reminder that we are enough. God made you just the way you are. He was intentional with you, not random. He didn't make you perfect, he made you unique. That's why I believe that God doesn't love us equally, God loves us uniquely. Because he knows us individually and fully. This love is a perfect love.

When John writes about this perfect love, he says, "There is no fear in love. But perfect love drives out fear, because fear has to do with punishment. The one who fears is not made perfect in love" (1 John 4:18). The Living Bible translates it this way: "We need have no fear of someone who loves us perfectly; his perfect love for us eliminates all dread of what he might do to us. If we are afraid, it is for fear of what he might do to us and shows that we are not fully convinced that he really loves us."

Did you catch that last line? If we are convinced that he doesn't really love us because we're not good enough to be loved, then we will always live in fear. But once this perfect love captures us, it conquers fear. In Greek, the word for "perfect" is *teleioō*, which means complete. Do you see the beauty of this? It's not just that God loves us completely, it's that God loves us with a love that is complete. God will never say, "You know, I love you more and more every day." God's love for us does not grow. It cannot grow any more. It is complete. God knows us intimately and loves us completely.

Imagine if you believed that from your very core. Would you be a different person? I know you would. You might not live in as much anxiety and fear. You would live more courageously and free. So I pray Paul's words over you: "May you have the power to understand, as all God's people should, how wide, how long, how high, and how deep his love is. May you experience the love of Christ, though it is too great to understand fully. Then you will be made complete with all the fullness of life and power that comes from God" (Ephesians 3:18-19 NLT).

Distorted Love

We live in fear because we don't know what love truly is. The kind of love we may be used to in relationships is not this divine love that makes us complete, but rather a deprived or depraved love. A deprived love is always lacking and is motivated by a sense of need. It's never satisfied and is always looking for someone to fill a void. That is why sometimes we get into unhealthy relationships and then stay in them. It's not that we don't realize they're not good for us. It's just that we have a need to be loved because we've been deprived of it.

Deprived love exists in families and friendships in which it's all about performance and behavior. We are given deprived love based on how much we can produce or how well we can accomplish things. It's connected to how we make other people feel. We want to be the ideal boyfriend or girlfriend. We want to be great kids for our parents. We want to be the perfect employee for our boss. We want to be the best parent a kid could ever have. Somehow we are convinced that if we were the perfect person we would be loved "perfectly." This leads to fear of failure.

Deprived love also convinces us that our net worth is connected to our sense of self-worth. We feel the need to be successful in order for people to love us. We feel the need to be important for people to admire us. We feel the need to be powerful for people to praise us. The worst thing we could do is fail. In our minds, we become unlovable because of our failures and flaws. What's worse is that we begin to love people the same way.

Another kind of love is depraved love. It is different from deprived love in that it has an agenda. Depraved love is corrupt. It has an alternative motive that seeks to manipulate. It is sinister and self-centered. It is when people use one another to get what they want, and love is used as bait. Sadly, sometimes people don't even know they are loving in this way. They've never encountered unconditional love, so they love with condition, and the condition is that they live for their needs and wants. Depraved love also plays games. It always keeps score and is always trying to get on top of the leaderboard. It leads to tit for tat—you-scratch-my-back-and-I'll-scratch-yours kind of relationships. These relationships are consumed with who is compromising more in the relationship versus creating a deeper relationship. These relationships are bound up in fear and anxiety. Deprived and depraved love leave us wanting more and needing to control.

How Love Frees Us from a Fear of Failure

God's perfect love frees us to love like him, to see people's flaws and faults through his eyes. It also enables us to see failure through a different lens, to see failure as a friend. Yes, failure is a better friend than success. Success flatters you and tells you what you want to hear. It tells you that there is nothing better than "him"—success. He is all you need. With him on your side you are irresistible and indestructible, free from the worries of the world. But success is a compulsive liar. He can't help himself. He is right about this one; he's the best wingman. He is the best plus-one. You and I can't deny that success is awesome to have around and always delivers on momentary pleasure.

However, failure is the friend that you need to have but don't like to admit you know. She is like that classmate you don't want to sit with at lunch. She is awkward and might embarrass you at times. But she is honest with you. She tells it to you like it is and does not pull any punches. At times she is harsh, but it's for your own good. Failure is a true friend—not warm and fuzzy, but she shows you how far you have come. She shows you if you are growing or not. She tests your potential. She is annoying. Sometimes you want to break up with her forever, get as far away from her as possible—maybe leave town without letting her know. You wonder if you should end it with a text or just ghost her. Nevertheless, she is a keeper. She is honest and committed to your growth. She wants you to fail at some things so that you can truly win in the most important things. I know it's a unique way to look at success and failure. But if we saw the depth of what failure does for us, failure would not be scary, and we would not have to fear failure.

God uses failure as a gardening tool for our growth. God loves to see growth. I'm convinced that is one of the reasons Jesus was born as baby, so God could see his Son grow. God loves to see us grow. He loves to watch us try and fail and learn. He enjoys seeing our determination to get better at things and mature in our understanding. If you've ever seen a toddler try to walk or a teenager finally getting her driver's license or a college student graduate, you know what I'm talking about. Jesus expounds on God's love of growth by saying:

> I am the true grapevine, and my Father is the gardener. He cuts off every branch of mine that doesn't produce fruit, and he prunes the branches that do bear fruit so they will produce even more. You have already been pruned and purified by the message I have given you. Remain in me, and I will remain in you. For a branch cannot produce fruit if it is severed from the vine, and you cannot be fruitful unless you remain in me. (John 15:1-4 NLT)

Fear of Failure

God knows who we are, and he loves us. God sees who we could be and prunes us, cutting away the things that are keeping us from growing into the people he created. Failing or losing can be a part of God's process to make us more fruitful. If you find yourself in the middle of your greatest failure, if you have lost precious relationships or opportunities, it could be that God is pruning you, cutting away some "branches"—some people or options—in your life. When we go through times like these, it's important that we are honest about our feelings. Losing hurts, and our souls were created to grieve. We need to allow ourselves to take a minute or as long as we need. But God is still with us. Failure is no longer to be feared.

Six

Fear of Rejection

Several years ago, I asked a celebrity to take a picture with me and was denied. It happened at a party. Although most people weren't paying attention, it felt like all eyes were on me when she said no. I can't really express the embarrassment and shame I felt. But I also remember experiencing anger and then, a few minutes later, feeling extremely insecure. I'm sure she had her reasons, but it didn't matter in the moment. It's not that I don't like to hear no, it's just that I already had a suspicion that I could be denied. I was trying to be brave when I asked; and the only reason I asked for a picture was for a friend who was a true fan of hers. Before I asked, I even explained that it was for a friend; I thought he would appreciate it. But apparently she didn't. The only saving grace is that she left the party right after our interaction—that and the fact that no one had actually overheard our conversation.

I had not felt that insecure in a long time. I had plenty of embarrassing and insecure moments growing up, but I had mostly avoided them as an adult. I think rejection hits differently as an adult; it might even send us back in time to make us feel like a child. It's an unsettling feeling that can shake us to our core.

Fear of Rejection   55

Unfortunately, it recently happened again. I was in a studio to record my first book, *Ex-Muslim,* on Audible. My publisher said it would be a good idea for me to read my own book. I had concerns because my dyslexia impairs my spelling and reading. It means my brain doesn't process spelling patterns or words in the right order, so I often read or say one word when I mean something similar. I informed the studio engineers of this before we started, and they seemed to be cool with it. After three hours and two chapters in, we took a break. That's when the guy who owned the studio asked me if I had considered hiring someone else to read the book.

I said, "Yes, I did, but the publisher was hoping I would read my own book."

After the break, we went for another hour or so and called it a day. It was painful for all of us, but I was encouraged by their desire to work with me—or so I thought. "Why don't you review the next three chapters for tomorrow and I'll see you in the morning," he said as I left for the day. I was discouraged but also grateful and hopeful.

The next morning, I drove up to the studio but noticed the lights inside were turned off. *Maybe they are running late,* I thought. But then I saw someone inside, so I knocked. The person came to the door like he was surprised to see me.

"Oh, did you not get the message? Your publisher is going in a different direction."

"Uh, okay, what do you mean?" I asked. "What happened?"

He then proceeded to tell me that right after I left the day before, my publisher emailed him that they were going in a different direction and didn't want to work on this project. I was confused but sensed that he was lying.

So I asked again, "So you are telling me that my publisher emailed you unexpectedly right after I left?"

"Yes, they did," he said, barely looking at me.

I sat in my car to breathe. I knew it had been a rough start trying to read my book. I knew that at times they were frustrated by my reading ability. But how did my publisher find out so fast? Did they change their mind about me? I called them right there from my car outside the recording studio.

"We did not email him; he emailed us yesterday and said he did not want to work on this project," explained my publisher. "I'm so sorry, are you okay?"

He was very kind to ask. Honestly, I didn't know; I hated this feeling. It was a very real reminder that I have a disability—a disability that I don't like to face. It's not a matter of effort; I have tried my whole life to get better. I make my living as a public speaker. I have to read out loud in front of hundreds, if not thousands of people all the time. So I'm committed to improving my skills; but it's a disability that is out of my control. I can't read two or three sentences at once perfectly. I will creatively change or add words to the sentence. It works for public speaking but apparently it does not work when you are recording an audiobook.

His lie exposed my truth: I have a disability. His cowardly rejection of me left me cowering.

The Longing to Be Admired

We all dislike rejection because it brings up emotional stuff that no one wants to deal with. So the best way is to never, ever put ourselves in a place where we will be rejected. Right? Wrong! It's a place where we can be in control, but it is a very unsatisfying place. It means we only start projects, take opportunities, get into

Fear of Rejection 57

relationships if we can control the outcome. We think it sets us up for guaranteed success but doing so denies us the chance to experience something bigger than ourselves.

One day a friend said to me, "Naeem, I think you would rather be admired than known." These words have bugged me for years. I knew he meant well. He was a friend—and I say "was" because I unfriended him that day (just kidding). His statement was true and, like most honest words, it was uncomfortable.

I have always liked being the person that everybody likes, that everyone finds interesting and charming. It might be because I'm an Enneagram Three. If you're not familiar with the Enneagram, do yourself a favor and read about it. Believe me, it will help you understand your personality and how to navigate all your relationships. It helped me understand my core needs and fears. The fear of rejection is very real for my personality type. I fear that people would reject me if they truly knew me. My personality also likes to win. When you put these two traits together, you can see why I would rather be admired than known. No one rejects people they admire.

Another area of rejection for me was the color of my skin. "He is so dark," my mom said to my aunt when I was born, comparing me to my much lighter-skinned older brother. Being light-skinned in Pakistani culture is considered attractive and beautiful. My mom said that several people expressed condolences about my coloring. She did have two sons. My brother and I were her first and second born. But people told her, "you can't have it your way all the time," and "Allah has already blessed you once."

Fair & Lovely is a skin-lightening cream common in Indian and Pakistani cultures. There is this idea that we need to be attractive

58 PART TWO: TODAY IS WAITING

to be wanted, and Fair & Lovely made that happen. We needed to be a certain kind of person if we wanted people to accept us.

What kind of culture did you grow up in? Did you grow up in a home where you had to be a certain kind of person? With a particular personality? Or did you live in a home where they were waiting for you to get better? Did you grow up feeling that at any point you could be rejected if you brought your whole self to the relationships you were in? This might be the reason some of us find ourselves in relationships in which we're not completely ourselves— we feel that if people truly knew us they would reject us.

Jesus Understands Us

The fear of rejection is one that Jesus was familiar with. If Jesus— the author and finisher of our faith, the one we look to, the one who showed us how to live a life of character and confidence, the person we need to emulate in every way—lived with rejection himself, then we have to get comfortable with it too.

Isaiah wrote this about Jesus:

He had no beauty or majesty to attract us to him,
    nothing in his appearance that we should desire him.
He was despised and rejected by mankind,
    a man of suffering, and familiar with pain.
Like one from whom people hide their faces
    he was despised, and we held him in low esteem.
        (Isaiah 53:2-3)

This passage in the Old Testament is what was prophesied about Jesus. But the New Testament talks about what in fact did happen to Jesus. Here is one description in Matthew 8:34 (NASB 1995): "And behold, the whole city came out to meet Jesus; and when they

Fear of Rejection 59

saw Him, they implored Him to leave their region." Imploring him to leave feels like rejection, doesn't it? Have you ever been implored to leave? What is so wild about this is that it's right after Jesus had healed a demon-possessed guy.

Have you ever done the right thing, only to be rejected because of it? Have you ever been there for people, but when the tables were turned, they were not there for you? Have you wanted to hold on to a relationship or friendship even after the other person made it clear that they were done? Have you ever just wanted closure in a relationship, yet you find that you're still waiting for it? Being ghosted by someone you had a significant relationship with lingers in your soul a lot longer than a relationship that ended sadly but properly.

There's not much I can relate to when it comes to the level of rejection that Jesus experienced. For example, take this passage: "They got up, forced Jesus out of town, and took him to the edge of the cliff on which the town was built. They planned to throw him off the edge" (Luke 4:29 NCV). I don't think I've ever experienced people being so bothered by me that they wanted to throw me off a cliff (maybe my parents when I was a teenager, but they would have never done it—I hope). Yet, as I read these words I find myself at peace with the idea that Jesus understands rejection. Jesus relates to us. But in this verse in John, I find myself being able to relate to Jesus: "He came to His own, and those who were His own did not receive Him" (John 1:11 NASB 1995).

Jesus does not just pity me. He has compassion for me. He has empathy for me. He has been there. He knows how it feels and how it shakes your confidence, but he also knows that how we relate to rejection will shape our character. It might be because of the person you are, your ideas, or your ideals. Maybe it's the kind

60 PART TWO: TODAY IS WAITING

of people you're surrounding yourself with. People can reject us for any or all of these reasons.

It's hard for me to say this, and even harder for me to do: do not fear rejection. Brain imaging research suggests that the pain of rejection and physical pain are actually processed in similar ways by our brain. That is why it seems like my heart hurts when someone rejects me. Learning to handle rejection profoundly strengthens our soul and grows our character. A great rejection by others can lead to a greater acceptance of self. When rejected, our response is key. Although it's so hard to control our immediate response, we can choose to be intentional as we process it. Greater intimacy, vulnerability, and resilience can come from rejection when our response is to share our pain with others, to name the emotions we are feeling, and to choose to learn from it.

Although rejection can feel like a slammed door in our face, it can open up new opportunities and possibilities. Luke 17 tells us that Jesus' rejection had not only a hidden meaning but a higher meaning to it. Here's what Luke says: "But first He must suffer many things and be rejected by this generation" (Luke 17:25 NASB 1995). Rejection was part of the plan when it came to the life Jesus would live and eventually give up for us.

It is common in my culture to be spoken for early on in life. I was sort of spoken for when I was born. I was supposed to marry my cousin. Growing up, interacting with the cousin was so awkward for both of us. Can you imagine us as teenagers trying to interact knowing what we knew? But when the time came my mom decided to say no to arranging my marriage. I'm so grateful for that no! Even though that no was the main reason my relatives looked down on me, I felt such relief. My mom's rejection of that plan created freedom for me. She created opportunity and possibility by

Fear of Rejection 61

saying no to my relatives. She was the one who rejected and then, in turn, was rejected by her relatives. I can only imagine what life would look like if I were destined to a fate I did not choose.

Choosing to accept no is powerful. Being comfortable with saying no is freeing.

It's hard for me to receive rejection and to hear a no, and it's also hard for me to say no. "You say okay to everything," my wife, Ashley, reminds me. It's true. I have such an aversion to rejection that I don't ever want to reject anybody or anything. So I will say yes to invitations and opportunities to people that I don't really want to say yes to. It's a problem; it's not fair to people, and it's not healthy for me.

Are you living your life in a certain way right now simply because you don't want to say no? Because you fear hurting people, could it be you're hurting yourself? Gaining a healthy, positive view of rejection by learning to set good boundaries with others is going to allow us to move our lives forward. The fear of rejection, failure, and loss can keep us from the life that God wants us to live. It might even paralyze us to move forward. For some of us, fear has kept us captive. But the future is calling.

What does it look like to conquer fear of your present or your past to create a beautiful future? Let's find out together.

Part Three

Tomorrow Needs You

Hope is the possibility of a beautiful tomorrow.

The world is better because you are in it. This is an undeniable truth that needs to solidify in your soul. These are words I have told my kids often and will continue to remind them because our failures and fears can make us forget. Sometimes our disillusionment and depression can make us think thoughts like, *Does this world really need me? Nobody will miss me if I'm gone. No one cares that much about me. The world would be better if I was not in it.* Even though it's tempting to believe these thoughts in the midst of despair, they are lies, trying to rob you of your tomorrow.

Yesterday might have been disappointing and disorienting. It might have been tragic, sad, or ugly. It might have caused you to doubt your importance. You may wonder if things will ever get better or if you are needed in this world.

But your tomorrows and other people's tomorrows truly need you. There are people in your life that need you to be present in their tomorrows—their futures.

So, let's arm ourselves with hope—a divine hope that does not disappoint. We can learn to create tomorrow for ourselves and our loved ones.

Seven

When Faith Fails

This can't be real, I thought to myself as I read an email for TEDx Charlotte.

Like most of us, I have received my share of junk and scam emails. I have disappointed a few rich Nigerian princes who desperately needed my help to transfer funds. But these days it's getting harder to discern what is legit. This specific email was inviting me to audition to speak at an upcoming TEDx conference.

Well, there is no money involved. Should I click the link to fill out the form? I began reasoning. *What should I do?* I needed help. My wife, Ashley, is the sole reason I have not made some seriously dumb decisions in my life, so I called out, "Ash, come check this out."

"Looks pretty legit to me; let's look at the form." Her words gave me the courage to proceed.

It was a big deal for me to consider applying to be a speaker. Remember, I don't love rejection. I didn't want to get my hopes up just for it to turn out to be a dud. The thought of being rejected after applying felt like a palpable possibility. And then there was the most apparent dilemma: what is my "idea worth sharing"?!

66 PART THREE: TOMORROW NEEDS YOU

Soon after submitting my idea, I received another email. "I got accepted!" I blurted out in excitement to Ashley. "They want me to come in for the second round, an in-person audition!"

As much as I was experiencing excitement in that moment, fear walked into my mind. Fear strolled in, talking within me: *Being rejected in person is going to be humiliating. Do you really want to do this?* I heard the voice of fear, but I fought against it.

Two weeks later, I drove to the audition, and when I arrived at the location, I sat in my car for a minute to get in the zone. *Why are you doing this? You don't need to do this. Why are you putting yourself through this? Is your idea truly an idea worth sharing?* Fear was back because it loves to hear itself speak.

I'm doing this, I reminded my soul. *Jesus, I believe that you set this up and you will be with me. If I'm wrong, then at least I failed trying to obey you.*

Sitting in the hallway waiting to walk into the room for my turn to audition triggered a memory. Although I was an adult, I felt like that twelve-year-old waiting in the principal's office. Was it because I had heard "You will always be a failure"? I'm sure it was. It's hard to erase words like those spoken over you. If you battle with brutal words that have been spoken over you, I can relate. I don't know if it gets easier, but I know that you can get stronger.

"We are ready for you," Jill, one of the TEDx organizers, said, interrupting my thoughts.

"Oh, okay," I said, rising to my feet. As I walked into the room, I had no idea what to expect. There were four people already in the room. *Four! Come on, why four? I'm really good one-on-one, or even one-on-two, but four? This is going to be hard,* I thought to myself.

"Whenever you are ready," the woman said.

"Okay, so I just start?" I asked.

When Faith Fails 67

"Yeah," she answered. I was hoping for something more—you know, some small talk to make me more comfortable. But they were ready to go. The good thing was that their faces communicated kindness, which is rare in this world.

So I took a deep breath and said, "I'm Naeem Fazal. I believe that beauty is the solution to fear. It is the beautiful things in our lives that have the power to conquer the fearful things in our lives."

The rest is a blur. It was a ten-minute talk, but it felt like ten seconds. I finished just in time before my body began to sweat with all the nervous energy.

"Thank you, Naeem, for coming in," one of them said.

"Okay . . . well . . . thank you!" I replied, hoping for a hint to how I did. *Was I in?* I wondered. *I think I nailed it; I think.* I continued to deliberate with myself as I drove back home. Six months later, I took the stage at TEDx Charlotte. Afterward, my "idea worth sharing" became a conviction worth living. My idea empowered me to use my beautiful goal to push through my fear and anxiety. What if you did the same?

Fighting the Fear That Holds Us Back

Have you ever thought that you were several different people—the person you want to be or the person you wish could be, and the person you actually are? You have an image of the happy, fulfilled, courageous, and kind person you could be. What is keeping you from it? What is keeping you from the career you want or the person you want to date? How do we fight against the fears that are holding us back?

In the previous chapters, we have talked about the reality of fear. We talked about our how fears are vividly real and unique to us. These fears, if left unbridled, will keep us from living the life we want to live, the life we are meant to live. How can we set aside fear? In this chapter we begin to look outside ourselves for a way forward.

"*Bismallah*'—remember to say it," my mother told me, trying to comfort me when I was scared of the dark. As a kid, I would often get afraid at night. I wanted to sleep in my parents' bed most nights. The phrase she told me to repeat at night translates in English as "In the name of Allah." Muslims, like Catholics, have their own rosary, a string of beads for keeping count. Just like Catholics are prescribed "Hail Marys," Muslims have Islamic phrases for provisions from Allah. Repeating these phrases was a way to conquer fear. Sometimes we would wear necklaces that would have a page of the Qur'an wrapped in cloth as a pendant. This was the way I was taught to conquer my fears as a child.

I grew up with Hindus from India. Arvind was one of my best friends growing up, and he still is today. Because of him and his loving family, I witnessed "puja," Hindu worship. Hindus share a common conviction (or superstition, depending on who you are asking) called "the evil eye." The evil eye represented bad omens or bad luck. It could be an evil presence or a fearful spirit. If you see a Hindu wearing a red thread bracelet, it's probably a talisman to ward off evil.

In most religions, faith is offered as the solution to fear. The Christian religion is no different. A heavier dose of faith is often prescribed to combat fear. We hear it in sermons and sing it in our worship songs. But does it work? Is it making us more faith-filled and less fearful people? An encounter I had at church comes to mind when I think about someone who is locked in this belief system.

When Faith Fails 69

Controlled by Fear

"I'm sorry," the woman said, apologizing for crying as she was talking to me.

"It's okay. What's wrong?" I asked, trying to comfort her. I knew who she was. She and her husband had been attending Mosaic for a few months. I looked at her husband, trying to gauge what was happening. I was in full pastor mode in that moment.

"Well, I don't know how to say it—" she tried to explain, wiping away tears.

I was about to say something comforting, but then she let it out.

"I think you are a sleeper terrorist." She continued to explain how she and her husband had been followers of Jesus for a long time and had loved their experience at Mosaic. But she was struggling with the fear that I was going to invade the evangelical church and then . . . honestly, I don't remember exactly what she said after that. Part of the problem was that I wasn't sure if she was confessing or wanting me to come clean. And frankly, I didn't know if I should pray for her or have pity for her, because it felt like I got punched in the stomach. Needless to say, I was not ready for that confession.

"Oh, okay. Well, I'm not," I responded, not knowing what to say. "It's okay. Do you still feel that way?"

I was still so stunned that I don't even remember her answer. But I do remember that she and her husband eventually left our church. To their credit, they did serve and support for a while after that awkward conversation.

What burdened me the most was how a person of faith, a follower of Jesus, could allow fear to control her quality of life.

Faith is the opposite of fear, but it is not the solution to fear. This woman's faith alone didn't allow her to see me as a person made in

God's image. Faith helps us see God's goodness, but beauty reveals the goodness in people. When we see the beauty in people, it releases us from fear of people. Our fears cause distrust, which allows us to justify prejudice.

Some people believe we just need to have more faith to fight against fears in our life. We just need to trust more to fight against the trauma in our life. People ask us to be more courageous, to be more positive; but that is not enough. We need something bigger in front of us to dismantle the fears within us.

Regardless of the fears we have—fear of loss, pain, failure, regret, shame, guilt—the solution to fear is not faith. Faith is just the opposite of fear. Faith is what we do in spite of our fears. What, then, will be our motivation to move forward regardless of our insecurity and uncertainty?

Look to the Beauty of Jesus

Our motivation has to be the beautiful thing we have in front of us. To call something or someone beautiful is to hold that thing or person in a higher—bigger—regard. If we hold Jesus before us, we will be able to put our faith in action to conquer the fears that paralyze us.

Jesus shows us how: "For the joy set before him he endured the cross" (Hebrews 12:2). Jesus saw a beautiful humanity that was worth dying for. That joy gave him the power to give his life, to "drink the cup of suffering." The writer of Hebrews explains it:

> Therefore, since we are surrounded by such a great cloud of witnesses, let us throw off everything that hinders and the sin that so easily entangles. And let us run with perseverance the race marked out for us, fixing our eyes on Jesus, the pioneer and perfecter of faith. For the joy set before him he endured

When Faith Fails 71

the cross, scorning its shame, and sat down at the right hand of the throne of God. (Hebrews 12:1-2)

"Fixing our eyes on Jesus" sets the joy in front of us that will conquer the fear within us. This is important to understand, because so many of us feel like we need to muster up this ethereal substance called faith to somehow gain God's favor and possess what we are praying for. We've been told faith is the answer to fear, but it is the joys—the beautiful hopes, dreams, relationships, and moments in our lives—that have power to overcome our fears. They empower us to be brave and courageous. These joys are the fruit of our life in Christ, fueling our faith and energizing our endurance.

King David, the second king of ancient Israel, seems to have understood this when he wrote, "I have set the LORD always before me; because He is at my right hand I shall not be moved" (Psalm 16:8 NKJV). King David dealt with intense fears and anxiety for about seven years as King Saul hunted him down from one end of the land Israel to the other. After David was chosen to be king, it took him about fifteen years to become king. Can you imagine the thoughts David struggled with? Every day came with new insecurities and worries about whether he would ever be king and could handle the responsibilities.

Personally, I fear that people might not like a post I make on social media; my extent of "persecution" from haters is a negative and critical comment. But David had a king literally hunting him down. David must have learned early on the importance of putting joy in front of him. He was intent to keep his eyes fixed on beautiful things.

Discover Joy

In Psalm 8 David shows us his perpetual practice of seeking beauty:

> When I look at your heavens, the work of your fingers,
>   the moon and the stars, which you have set in place,
> what is man that you are mindful of him,
>   and the son of man that you care for him?
> Yet you have made him a little lower than the
>   heavenly beings
> and crowned him with glory and honor.
>   (Psalm 8:3-5 ESV)

I have adopted this practice as well. I often take long walks at night to look up and put beauty in front of me. When life gets hard, when worry wears me out and fear wants to drag me into depression, I go out and look up to see the greatness of God. I get overwhelmed with the goodness of God that has followed me all the days of my life. God's Spirit reminds me of all the beautiful things in my life, and my fear is forced to surrender to God's love.

Do you find yourself in moments when you are overwhelmed with dread? Or in seasons in which you are submerged in sadness? Are you being terrorized by the trauma of your past? Do you have it in you to fight another day, or are you running on empty? I need you to hear me: you are not alone. I need you to see the beauty around you and the beautiful tomorrow that lies ahead of you.

As we leave this chapter to explore your future, I want to leave you with my favorite quote from a poem by Sarah Williams called "The Old Astronomer to His Pupil": "Though my soul may set in darkness, it will rise in perfect light; / I have loved the stars too fondly to be fearful of the night."

Eight

Why Beauty?

"Islam mein ye Haram hai," she said, discouraging me from drawing portraits of people. I had just shown my mom a drawing I was working on. It was *Haram* (a sin), forbidden in Islam, to draw portraits of real people. I asked why.

"Because you capture a part of their soul if you draw their face," she explained in Urdu.

This might be strange for some, but for that reason alone I grew up with no photos of loved ones on the walls of our house. Maybe that is why I have always loved the faces of people—not that I wanted to sin, but rather I wanted to capture the essence of a person. I loved (and still love) attempting to capture and communicate a part of who someone is in a painting. I want my portraits to make the viewer feel something about the person. In college I originally wanted to be an art major because I love beauty. I ended up majoring in corporate communications, which I felt would help me follow my calling to ministry.

We call people beautiful when we find ourselves personally attracted to them. Something is beautiful to us when we find it appealing. "Beauty is in the of the eye of the beholder" we say. So something that is beautiful to one person might not be beautiful to another.

When we are captivated by beauty, we are convinced that its value is lofty, vast, and substantial. I believe this unique quality of beauty makes it the perfect opponent against fear. I'm convinced that when I put a beautiful, bigger thing before me, it gives me the power to conquer the biggest fears in front of me. In contrast, we diminish the value of things we don't consider beautiful. The problem with this is that when we think our lives are not beautiful, we devalue our worth.

Beauty Inspires Us to Dream

History shows us men and women who also dreamed of a better, more beautiful humanity, and who fearlessly gave up their lives for it. For example, Mohandas Karamchand Gandhi was an Indian lawyer, anticolonial nationalist, and political ethicist who, among other things, inspired movements for civil rights and freedom across the world. He led several hunger strikes against religious violence. He is often quoted as having said, "Our ability to reach unity in diversity will be the beauty and the test of our civilisation." Tragically, he was assassinated at an interfaith prayer meeting in 1948. He had a beautiful vision of diverse people living in unity. Gandhi believed in the beauty of what could be, but he also saw the beauty in all of the people around him.

At eleven years old, Malala Yousafzai, a Pakistani student, wrote an anonymous diary about how she dreamed of girls being able to go to school. Her beautiful dream inspired a lot of people but opposed the Taliban, a militant Pashtun nationalist organization in Afghanistan. They had put a ban on education for girls.

Why Beauty? 75

Because of what Malala said in her diary, in October 2012 she was shot by their soldiers; but she survived the attack. At fourteen, she became the youngest person ever to win the Nobel Peace Prize.

Thomas Peschak, a marine biologist turned photographer turned activist, once shared how frustrated and outraged he was by certain natives who were killing marine life in the oceans. He began to take pictures that showed the horror of their actions, but nothing changed. He then started taking beautiful pictures, capturing and showing the beauty of the ocean and incredible marine life that lived there. They stopped. They changed their fishing practices. "Beauty changed them," Peschak explained in his TED Talk.

From prison inmates to people suffering from PTSD and other illnesses, creating and exploring beauty has proved to heal the spirit, soul, and body. It empowers us to dream and create a better future.

Ten years before he passed away, my dad had quadruple bypass surgery. It scared him so much that he didn't want to drive or do anything that might elevate his heart rate. He allowed the voice of fear to enter his mind, and it began to eat away at his soul to the point he couldn't see anything beautiful worth living for. Doctors would tell him that, even more than medication and rehab, he needed a reason to live. Beauty could have saved my dad. Beauty possesses hope, the possibility of a better tomorrow. However, my dad didn't have a beautiful dream for himself or for his family to help him push past his fears. That's why he attempted suicide. This is what I know: fear might control our emotions, but beauty has the power to shape our souls. It seems like fear knows that it can be conquered by beauty.

Tyrants use fear to oppress a culture by destroying its beauty. I saw it firsthand when Iraq invaded Kuwait in the Gulf War as Saddam Hussein began bombing beautiful landmarks—even a mosque—to instill fear and control. As the war continued and as Saddam Hussein saw he was losing, he began to destroy and remove anything that Kuwaitis considered precious or beautiful to their legacy.

Prejudice and racism exist in our culture because we fail to see beauty in people who are not like us. But when we can appreciate others, it conquers our concerns about them. Seeing beauty takes time. It's only when we sit and spend time with people who are not like us that we begin to perceive their profound uniqueness. It's no wonder that people who are quick to stand on issues rarely sit with people.

The Beauty of Humanity

There is a lot that is wrong in the world. We see the ugliness of humanity when people are mistreated and abused. We see the ugliness in relationships when people who made vows to love each other betray and belittle each other. We see the ugliness of corporate greed in unfair wages and unjust practices. We see the ugliness of our culture when prejudice and systemic racism are ignored, excused, and justified. And then there is the ugliness of disease and illness. It is unbearable to see loved ones deteriorate and die. Looking at all the ugliness can cause us to become cynical and pessimistic. It tempts us to be doubtful and skeptical that things can change let alone become beautiful.

Jesus saw the beauty in humanity—even in those who were steeped in the ugliness of the world. Zacchaeus the tax collector is

Why Beauty? 77

an example of someone who was transformed when Jesus saw him in a new way. Luke tells us about Zacchaeus:

> Jesus entered Jericho and was passing through. A man was there by the name of Zacchaeus; he was a chief tax collector and was wealthy. He wanted to see who Jesus was, but because he was short he could not see over the crowd. So he ran ahead and climbed a sycamore-fig tree to see him, since Jesus was coming that way. (Luke 19:1-4)

Luke tells us that Zacchaeus was not a guy who was liked by most people because he was part of the problem that plagued the Jewish people. In Greek, Zacchaeus means "pure" or "innocent," which is ironic because he was anything but that based on his actions. Zacchaeus, as a chief tax collector for the vicinity of Jericho, was a Jew who took advantage of his own people by cheating the elderly and exploiting the working poor. He was also considered by some to be a traitor to the political cause. In rabbinical literature, tax collectors are akin to robbers. Needless to say, most people didn't see anything beautiful about Zacchaeus. But Jesus did, because God sees not only our problematic past but also our potential future. God sees the beauty that is in us today.

Notice what happened next: "When Jesus reached the spot, he looked up and said to him, 'Zacchaeus, come down immediately. I must stay at your house today'" (Luke 19:5).

"I must stay at your house"—talk about inviting yourself over. It was as if Jesus was saying, "I need to be around you. There is something I see in you that I'm drawn to." Zacchaeus came down at once and welcomed Jesus gladly. "All the people saw this and began to mutter, 'He has gone to be the guest of a sinner'" (Luke 19:7). Obviously all the other people didn't see what Jesus saw.

We don't know what happened at dinner, but we do know that beautiful gesture of Jesus' presence transformed Zacchaeus. Luke does tell us that, at the end of the dinner, "Zacchaeus stood up and said to the Lord, 'Look, Lord! Here and now I give half of my possessions to the poor, and if I have cheated anybody out of anything, I will pay back four times the amount'" (Luke 19:8).

Jesus showed Zacchaeus his misuse of his privilege. He was stealing from his own marginalized people by overtaxing them for his personal profit. But Jesus' beautiful act illuminated Zacchaeus to see not only who he had become but also how he had the potential to be more. That is why grace is so beautiful, because it is an invitation to be more, not do less. Beautiful grace doesn't excuse our bad behavior, but gives us yet another opportunity to be more than we can be.

Jesus ends the story of Zacchaeus with this: "Today salvation has come to this house, because this man, too, is a son of Abraham. For the Son of Man came to seek and to save the lost" (Luke 19:9-10). Can you imagine being in the room in that beautiful moment as Jesus restores Zacchaeus not only to God but to his own people?

Created Beautiful

There is plenty of ugly to go around. Beauty is rare. That is why we have to create it, for ourselves and for others in our world. In fact, beauty is what God wants for us; it's what he is doing in us and through us. We were created beautiful. Our creation account in Genesis 1:27 (NLT) proves it: "So God created human beings in his own image. In the image of God he created them; male and female he created them."

He made us with himself in mind. We are beautifully complex and intricate as revealed in Ephesians 2:10 (VOICE, emphasis

Why Beauty? 79

original): "For we are the product of His hand, *heaven's poetry etched on lives*, created in the Anointed, Jesus, to accomplish the good works God arranged long ago." We were created in beauty, but sin broke in and broke us. Now we are the broken becoming beautiful because of God's Son, Jesus. And we are the broken called to create beauty because of God's power, his Holy Spirit.

Nine

What Do You See?

"Naeem, meri aankhon se dekho."

Seriously, Mom?! I thought. I had heard that phrase before. It was her most popular phrase. This time it was some obscure article of clothing that she was in search of for a seamstress project. As I mentioned before, my mom is a seamstress—and a pretty amazing one. She is highly creative and has always found new ways to solve clothing-alteration problems, but apparently she was unable to find a new phrase. It was her most popular message and her favorite phrase to use: *"Meri aankhon se dekho."* It means "Look with my eyes."

"I don't have your eyes, Mom," I would say under my breath. It was annoying at times how she always said it when I was looking for something that was important to me. Growing up, I was always looking for something, usually something I needed for school. I have to admit, even now I constantly find myself looking for things I have misplaced. Can you relate? "Look with my eyes." What an interesting idea! How differently were my mom's eyes looking that my eyes couldn't see? Her eyes were looking to find; her eyes were expectant. Her eyes were also sure to find, confidently determined that regardless of the context she would recognize what she was

What Do You See? 81

looking for. My mom's eyes were clear; her sight was not fogged by the past. The past was where things were supposed to be, where they had been before. So her expectant, confident, and clear eyes always saw and found what she was looking for.

Are you looking for something you can't seem to find? Are you unable to see because you are not looking with the right eyes?

"Usako annkh lag gaye hai" is another common Pakistani phrase my mom uses. It's a hard one to translate literally into English because it would not make much sense. A literal translation would read "He has got the Eye." Getting "the Eye on you" in our culture is a bad thing. It's like saying that an evil eye has focused on you. A basic explanation of the evil eye is "the supernatural belief in a curse brought about by a malevolent glare, usually inspired by some evil intent." The belief in the evil eye among humans has existed throughout human history. Some cultures have used amulets, talismans, or specific plants to protect against it.

In the Muslim culture I was raised in, saying the phrase *"Masha Allah"* ("God has willed it") alongside a compliment prevents the compliment from attracting the evil eye. It would be like knocking on wood after saying something hopeful. My mom still believes this and always says *"Masha Allah."*

Seeing with the Eyes of Jesus

Jesus seems to be more concerned about our own eyes. "The eye is the lamp of your body; when your eye is clear, your whole body also is full of light; but when it is bad, your body also is full of darkness" (Luke 11:34 NASB 1995). Matthew says that Jesus continued the thought by explaining, "If your eye is bad, your whole body will be full of darkness. If then the light that is in you is darkness, how great is the darkness!" (Matthew 6:23 NASB 1995).

Jesus reminds us that the ability of our eyes to see is connected to the condition of our soul. A person who is filled with negativity like doubt, envy, disappointment, anger, or hatred will see the world differently than the person filled with positivity like grace, faith, hope, love, and empathy. He also understands the things that have darkened our souls. Sometimes it's sin, unhealthy destructive beliefs, or behaviors we have allowed in. Sometimes it's fear, paralyzing thoughts permitted to run wild in our minds. Sometimes it's grief, unprocessed sadness that has cemented itself in our hearts. Whatever the darkness is, it blurs and distorts our vision.

Jesus reminds us that our eyes are the window to the soul, but our eyes also project what is in our heart. Jesus is telling us that to see what God has for us, we have to look with his eyes. We spend our lives looking for things we can or can't see. Paul's prayer for the church in Ephesus was that "the eyes of your heart may be enlightened, so that you will know what is the hope of His calling, what are the riches of the glory of His inheritance" (Ephesians 1:18 NASB 1995). We need to see with Jesus' eyes.

If our tomorrow is blurry, then we begin by asking Jesus to show us today more clearly. So what do you see? Could there be a happier, more hopeful, more beautiful tomorrow? What is keeping you from seeing tomorrow in the light of God's love? Although we can't see all that God sees, is there something God wants to show you that you are not seeing?

A traumatic car accident made it hard for Jason to see in new situations. "Even now, all these years later, I still freeze just a little when I see brake lights in front of me. I instantaneously glance at the rearview mirror. My body tenses up, and I am bracing for impact, fully convinced that car behind me is going to slam into my car," Jason confessed. "I have had to pull off the side of the road

What Do You See? 83

and take a minute." Jason's vulnerability reminds us that we need to give ourselves grace and space to heal from our past.

What about you? Do you have triggering moments that cause you to freeze up and fog up your vision? Moments in which you can't truly see what is going on?

Seeking Encouragement

I got glasses when I was eleven years old. My nearsightedness has continued to get worse and worse over the years. At thirty-three years old, I got LASIK eye surgery, and it was 20/20 vision from then on—until it was not. Apparently, LASIK only lasts forever if you don't age. Unfortunately, I'm not a vampire, and so seventeen years later I needed glasses again. If I choose not to wear them, things get unclear. But the main issue is my depth perception, which is worse at night when it's dark.

In life, we can't see the true depth of options when we can't see clearly. It's hard for all of us to see in the dark. How do you see when things in your life get dark, when gray, ominous clouds cover your days? Discouraging experiences have led to many seasons of disillusionment in my life. It's so hard for me to see the good and God things all around me when grief is within me. What has helped me is to have people who can point out things I am unable to see. At times we all need others to be our eyes because they can discern our blind spots.

"Naeem, look at all you have overcome and have accomplished." I still remember Chip's words. He was a fellow pastor who encouraged me to "see" all that was in my life.

The writer of Proverbs 13:12 says that "hope deferred makes the heart sick." I have seen this truth play out in my life. How about you? Are you in a dark place right now? The death of a dream or the dread of a diagnosis can dim the light in you. It can make your heart sick, but I believe it can also make your eyes weak.

Maybe God is asking you to go for a walk in the dark because he wants to show you something. That is what he did with Abram when he was discouraged about the future: "Then the LORD took Abram outside and said to him, 'Look up into the sky and count the stars if you can. That's how many descendants you will have!'" (Genesis 15:5 NLT). I wish that we could see the stars in daylight, but it is on the darkest night that we see the stars shine so bright. Richard Rohr, in his book *The Naked Now*, suggests that it is great suffering that brings us back to God. He believed that great suffering allows humans to be more susceptible to God's Spirit.

Paul the apostle seems to see the same thing. He said "when I am weak, then I am strong" because God told him, "My grace is sufficient for you, for my power is made perfect in weakness" (2 Corinthians 12:9-10). Paul's weakness allowed him to see God's presence with him and God's strength working in him and through him.

So look again! What do you see now?

Seeing Past Ourselves

Several years ago, I was in a Target aisle looking for something, but someone was looking at me. I could feel their eyes on me. As I glanced over I saw a lady who smiled at me and said "Hi!" The way she said it communicated that we knew each other, but for the life of me, I could not register who she was. She did look very familiar; I knew I knew her but didn't know from where.

"Starbucks!" she exclaimed as if she heard the whole conversation in my head.

"Oh, yeah!" I said sheepishly, slightly embarrassed I didn't recognize her. "You are out of context!" I tried to explain away my oversight.

As I drove away, I felt God ask me, "Do you recognize me out of context?"

Hold up! Wait! What? I felt myself say.

God's Spirit continued talking to me. "Naeem, you know what I look like in context. You know what I look like in certain situations or in certain people. But can you see me in peculiar people and painful problems?"

I know what God looks like in church services or in prayer meetings. I sense him in moments of worship and contemplation. I recognize him working in people, but do I recognize God in a person stumping out of a bar or in an intense corporate business meeting? Do I recognize God in the person next to me on the plane or in my online interactions?

No, I guess I don't, I thought back.

I hate to admit this, but self-centeredness is one of the reasons I fail to see God out of context. This form of pride pretends to protect us, but it blinds us to the activity of God. Time and time again, it has impaired me from seeing people's pain and God's purpose. It has also caused me to comprehend circumstances incompletely and incorrectly. Self-centeredness is one of those things we can't really see clearly in ourselves because it shows up in different ways. It can show up in meetings at work or in conversations with friends and family members, in full costume. Being overly opinionated or unwilling to change is pride just dressed up. Being overly sensitive or needing constant attention and affirmation is self-centeredness in disguise.

We are all guilty of self-centeredness because sometimes our pain causes us to focus on ourselves. But if we have sat in our pain, disappointment, or hopelessness long enough, it begins to affect our vision. When we are worn out by failure, our eyes get heavy and our vision gets blurry and we can't see God or others.

86 PART THREE: TOMORROW NEEDS YOU

So how do we learn to see God out of context? It starts by being self-aware instead of self-centered. Be self-aware of who you are. You are chosen. God wants to partner with you to help people. God blesses people through people. God wants to partner with you. Be available. Develop a practice of asking God how he wants to partner with you in a particular situation or moment. It's simple prayers like "God, I'm available. Holy Spirit speak to me, show me what I'm not seeing here." Be brave. Be willing to risk and start a conversation with a stranger. "Can I give you a mom hug?" It's what my wife, Ashley, said to a stranger in line at a grocery store after hearing that person tell the cashier that her life was so hard in that season that she wanted to crawl back in her mother's womb. That brave act of compassion was risky for my wife, hugging a stranger in the grocery store. But I can't help but think how healing it was for that person to be reminded of God's compassion and love that he was sending through Ashley. Just by hugging her.

I believe when we are aware, available, and brave, we can see God out of context, working in peoples' lives, calling us to partner with him.

Letting in the Light

Sometimes I think God dims the lights for us to really see things in a unique way. Lighting creates a mood and communicates intention. We see this in the ways grocery stores and classrooms are lit up versus how restaurants and coffee shops are. There's a huge difference between the lighting in your local post office versus the lighting in your local night club. Your gym is lit up to communicate something very different from that of the lighting in a cocktail lounge. Why am I bringing this up? Because I wonder if God uses

What Do You See? 87

the amount of light in a season of our lives to communicate his intention and will for our lives.

John 11 records the story of Jesus being confronted by Martha, who was distraught by the death of her brother Lazarus. Jesus was late getting there even though he knew Lazarus was in danger of dying. "Lord, if only you had been here, my brother would not have died. But even now I know that God will give you whatever you ask," Martha said to Jesus (John 11:21-22 NLT).

During the conversation Jesus tells her, "I am the resurrection and the life. Anyone who believes in me will live, even after dying. Everyone who lives in me and believes in me will never ever die. Do you believe this?" (John 11:25-26 NLT).

Jesus allowed the light of Martha's hope to be dimmed on purpose. God sometimes creates opportunities that cause doubt in order to create a deeper faith in him. That is why I'm convinced that doubt doesn't need to lead to disbelief, but rather can lead to a deeper faith in God.

The conversation ends with Martha saying, "Yes, Lord. . . . I have always believed you are the Messiah, the Son of God, the one who has come into the world from God" (John 11:27 NLT).

Is it hard for you to see God working in your life right now? When you look at your kids, do you get overwhelmed with a sense of dread because you are unable to perceive how things will turn around for them? When you look at your career, is it hard to distinguish how failure could result in forward momentum for you? When you look at your calendar for the month and there's a lack of any possible romantic dates or times with friends, is it hard for you to see joy?

Jesus put a joy before him, and that is what allowed him to endure the pain, the torture, the suffering of the cross. Jesus continually looked at the beauty of creation on purpose. Jesus looked for the good in people. Jesus was able to see potential in people that were considered problems to society. As Jesus grew up, like us, he had human eyes; but he also learned to see how his heavenly Father sees.

That is why Jesus, on purpose, attended weddings and funerals. He went to lavish parties and also had picnics in the park with a few thousand people. He saw humanity's successes and failures. He saw the betrayal in Judas' eyes and the denial in Peter's. He saw the overwhelming joy in Mary and Martha's eyes when Lazarus was resurrected from the dead. He saw the wonder and exhilaration in Thomas the disciple's eyes when he showed up in his resurrected body.

In all of this, Jesus chose to see something in us: a beautiful humanity that was worth living and dying for. He saw, like God, that the world was worth loving and sacrificing for, so that all of us would have a beautiful relationship with him.

Some people say that we see what we want to see. If this is true, then we have to courageously choose to truly see clearly, correctly, and fully. We cannot allow our current view of what is blind us to what could be. We cannot allow the brutality of this world to blind us to the beauty of this world.

So, what do you see? Will you join me in beholding beauty? Will you choose to believe that beauty has the power to dismantle the fear and anxiety in your life? Will you choose to focus ahead knowing that, regardless of your past or present, you can create a beautiful future?

Ten

A Beautiful Vision

"I'm not enrolled for the semester. Did they drop me?!" I was shocked, and sudden dread fell over me. "Why?" I asked, as my heart sank and my stomach dropped.

I had just finished my first semester at the College of Charleston (C of C). It was a big deal for me because I had recently come to the United States after being in the Gulf War. I had lost several years of education because I had only completed the eighth grade before Iraq invaded Kuwait. When you're living in a war-torn country, the importance of going to school is overridden by the need to stay safe. Even if they had wanted us to go to school, it wouldn't have been an option for me because my high school was destroyed during the war.

Needless to say, I did not have a high school diploma or a GED, but I had taken the TOEFL (Test of English as a Foreign Language). It is a standardized test to measure the English language ability of non-native speakers who wanted to enroll in English-speaking universities. Thankfully, I had done pretty well, which made it possible for me to get into C of C. But now it seemed that it was all over.

"Why did they do that?" I asked my brother Mahmood. "I passed all my classes last semester. So why?" He didn't say anything. It seemed like he knew the reason but did not want to give me the bad news. So I kept talking. "I know I enrolled for this semester; I picked all my classes weeks ago."

"I think it's the tuition fees," Mahmood ventured. He was right. The college canceled my classes because I had not finished paying for the previous semester.

I can't express in words how disappointing and depressing it was for me. I had worked so hard to get into college. My first semester was not just hard but humbling. I had to take English and math 90-level classes, not even the 101-freshman-level classes. It had also taken so long to get all my paperwork processed. I had a tourist visa that was expired. I had applied for an extension, but it was still unresolved. What I did not know was that Jesus was about to reveal himself to me and give me a beautiful vision for my life.

I often tell people that the night I met Jesus I found purpose. I still remember his words: "Your life is not your own." It wasn't a challenge but an invitation to live an incredible life. Those words were also reassuring that God was going to be in my life every step of the way. So, maybe I was naive, but I thought that he would miraculously clear the way for me since he was the one who called me to live a certain kind of life. I thought that going to college was his idea. I mean, I was terrified to go back to school. I knew it was going to be hell for me, but I also knew it was something that Jesus wanted me to do. So here I was trying to be obedient, hitting another obstacle.

Have you ever been stopped dead in your tracks and there seems to be no way forward? It often happens when we get news

A Beautiful Vision

that what we were hoping for is not possible—at least not the way we want it. The job doesn't pan out. The business deal falls through. The buyer backs out from the house closing. The relationship ends. Sometimes these endings feel like they are final. Sometimes these disappointments lead to disillusionment, especially when we've been praying and believing for them. And when heaven seems to be quiet, we begin to question ourselves. We wonder if God still counts us worthy of hearing and answering our heart's desires.

Believing That God Is Good

"It's because of my past, I know it is. It's because of all the things I have done." She could not even lift up her head to look up at me as she uttered these words. "That is why God will not let me have a baby," she continued as tears rolled down her cheeks and fell onto the floor.

I could only imagine the pain and desolation her barrenness had caused her. "No, Jane, God is not punishing you for your past. He doesn't do that." In that moment I was trying to be there for her as her pastor and friend. I wanted her to know that it was okay to feel all those feelings because God is not offended by our emotions. In fact, "we do not have a high priest who is unable to empathize with our weaknesses" (Hebrews 4:15).

But at that same time I also felt something else—a holy anger against the liar who was tempting her to doubt the goodness of God. Jesus said that when the devil lies "he speaks his native language, for he is a liar and the father of lies" (John 8:44).

"You are going to have a baby." I couldn't believe I said it out loud. I had a strong sense that it was going to happen, but I never want to make a promise like this to women who are struggling with infertility. *What are you saying,* I thought to myself. But I heard myself say it again, this time sure that it was going to happen. This is not something I do, have done since, or would recommend. Good intentions are not always great reasons to do things. But in that moment, I had an overwhelming sense of God's presence.

I was thrilled months later when she told me that she was indeed pregnant. Now, years later, she has several healthy kids!

I'm aware that this is not always the case. I have seen courageous women successfully pursue adoption because they had set a beautiful vision before them. I have seen other women shift their hearts toward caring for nieces and nephews or children in their community when having kids of their own wasn't an option. I've also seen a beautiful vision empower women to move from painfully waiting to faithfully trusting. They dreamed of nurturing and raising kids and were determined that their beautiful vision was worth the fight even if it wasn't ever going to play out like they originally dreamed or hoped.

A beautiful vision also dismantles the despair in our lives and fuels our faith to push through painful outcomes. For some of us, chronic worry or insecurity has led to despair because we have prayed and prayed and things are not working out. We feel disappointed at God and isolated, like we are all alone trapped in our pain. This is another place the enemy lurks and preys on our emotions, wanting us to believe that God has brought us to a painful place just to leave us there.

But I believe it is in moments like these that God wants to speak to us. He wants to give us a new vision that pushes us out of the past to create a new future. God wants to give us a new way forward.

A Beautiful Vision

Finding a Way Through

The next day, after realizing I had been dropped from my classes, I went to the admissions and treasurer office at the College of Charleston to plead my case. Unfortunately, there seemed to be no way around it. I had to come up with the money I owed before they would re-enroll me in my classes. It forced me to think about other ways to accomplish my vision and figure out how to pay off my tuition. I began to take classes at other local colleges. For the next few years, I took classes at two other colleges, while working two jobs. I worked three jobs in the summer when classes slowed down. When I finally transferred back to C of C, I asked for an appointment to talk with the president. I know, what in the world was I thinking? Did I really think I was going to get a meeting with him? Honestly, I thought, why not? Why couldn't he take a minute to talk with me?

The reason I wanted to have a meeting with him was to ask him to reduce my tuition. As an immigrant with religious refugee status, I was still considered an "international student," which meant that my fees were higher than that of even out-of-state students. I knew there was no way I could afford to pay that kind of money. Student loans weren't an option because of my status in the States. I believed I could convince the president if I could just have a conversation. So I started showing up to his office several times a week to see if he had the time. I would sit and do schoolwork for an hour or so, hoping that his office staff would have pity on me. It was very humbling, and I had to fight against rejection every time I sat there without being granted access to his office. But I was obsessed with the vision God had shown me for my life and that involved graduating from college.

"He will see you. You have five minutes." I couldn't believe what I was hearing. It was happening. I walked in trying to remember what I was going to say. I think I blanked. Thankfully, he started talking as soon as I entered his office.

"So my staff tells me that you have been hanging out by my office for weeks, trying to talk to me. What can I do for you?" He was a kind man, and that helped put me at ease. I took a breath and explained my situation.

"Well, you don't have the grades for academic scholarship, and you don't qualify for in-state tuition," he said, "but I'm going to make up a scholarship for you. Can you keep a 3.0 GPA?"

"Yes sir!" I nervously said. (You know by now that, for me, a 3.0 GPA would take a miracle.)

"You promise to graduate?"

"Yes sir!" I said with all the self-assuredness I could muster up. I will be forever grateful for his kindness, and I made sure to let him know when my graduation finally came.

So many people helped me along the way. Ashley, whom I was dating at the time, was one of those people. I didn't know about this until years later, but she would secretly go to the admissions office and deposit funds in my tuition account. For that reason and for so many more, she is now my wife.

What is your beautiful vision for the future that fills you with hope and purpose? What are the dreams and goals, the plans you believe God has put within you and before you?

What God Promises

"'For I know the plans I have for you,' declares the LORD, 'plans to prosper you and not to harm you, plans to give you hope and a future'" (Jeremiah 29:11). This passage is often quoted by people

A Beautiful Vision 95

who are looking for hope in an unclear future. I can see why. It reassures us of God's presence and intention when life gets complicated and things seem hopeless. But there's more to it than just well-meaning encouragement.

This was Jeremiah the prophet encouraging people who had been exiled to a foreign land, a period known as the Babylonian captivity or Babylonian exile. In this period of Jewish history, a large number of Jews from the ancient Kingdom of Judah were taken to Babylon, the capital city of the Neo-Babylonian Empire, after their defeat in the Jewish-Babylonian War. It is estimated that 10,000 to 20,000 people were removed from their land over a course of three different exiles. The first was in 597 BC during the reign of Jehoiachin, when Nebuchadnezzar attacked Jerusalem and plundered the temple and the royal palace. The second exile occurred after Jerusalem fell in 586 BC and the temple was destroyed. The third appears to have occurred around 582 BC while King Nebuchadnezzar once again exerted control over the region we know as Palestine.

These exiles were unexpected. After all, the Jewish people believed they had received a promise from God to protect them and use them for his purpose. I wonder if this crisis caused them to doubt if the promise had been misplaced. It probably caused cognitive dissonance to see that their expected future was not aligning with their reality. This kind of misalignment, when we can't reconcile what is with what should be, often leads to profound despair. They began to called themselves the *bene gola*, "the children of the exiled."

Texts like Ezekiel, Isaiah, Lamentations, Job, and much of Psalms are a result of these exiles. In fact, the story of Job illustrates one way the Jewish people processed the exile. Job, an upright man, is made to suffer the worst series of calamities until he finally finds restoration in the end.

It's in the midst of this that Jeremiah reminds his people that God has plans for them—a plan for good, not harm. A plan filled with purpose and promise. But that popular verse is actually the words Jeremiah ends with. He starts his charge to them like this:

> This is what the LORD of Heaven's Armies, the God of Israel, says to all the captives he has exiled to Babylon from Jerusalem: "Build homes, and plan to stay. Plant gardens, and eat the food they produce. Marry and have children. Then find spouses for them so that you may have many grandchildren. Multiply! Do not dwindle away! And work for the peace and prosperity of the city where I sent you into exile. Pray to the LORD for it, for its welfare will determine your welfare." (Jeremiah 29:4-7 NLT)

Plan to stay? Seriously! This is not what we want to hear when we are in a hard place in life. It is so disheartening to realize that staying in a hard season seems to be our reality. But notice that God is giving them a new vision, a new way forward. He wants them to take the beautiful vision of what could be and to get to work. I don't know about you, but when I find myself in a "Babylon season" I work hard to get out of it. The last thing I plan to be doing is to think about how I can work in it. Yet, God tells them to put their energy into creating—not coping—in an unexpected season. And I think he is telling us the same. Do it again is what God is essentially asking them to do. Build again, settle down again, put down roots again, make a living again, fall in love again, dream again, pray again, and trust God again. Doing it again is so hard.

A Beautiful Vision 97

We are constantly reminded of what was, which hinders us from reimagining what could be.

God continues through Jeremiah to say, "Do not let your prophets and fortune-tellers who are with you in the land of Babylon trick you. Do not listen to their dreams, because they are telling you lies in my name. I have not sent them" (Jeremiah 29:8-9 NLT).

What were the false prophets telling the people? They gave a false sense of expectancy and comfort. They were essentially saying that God was going to deliver them soon—"Any time now, God is going get you out of this season"—so the people didn't have to deal with the reality of their situation. They were saying that God was going to get them back to where they were, and that things were going to be just like they had been before. But that was a lie, a sweet lie that we would all be tempted to believe. Also, that sounds like something yesterday would tell us: just wait and see. Because yesterday wants us to get back to the past, to how things were. But God was telling them to work and create the future.

The false prophets were tempting the people to wonder about yesterday, wait on tomorrow, and waste today. But God's vision—a beautiful one—was calling the people to forget yesterday because tomorrow needs them and today is waiting on them. That is when Jeremiah ends with this:

> This is what the LORD says: "You will be in Babylon for seventy years. But then I will come and do for you all the good things I have promised, and I will bring you home again. For I know the plans I have for you," says the LORD. "They are plans for good and not for disaster, to give you a future and a hope." (Jeremiah 29:10-11 NLT)

Could there be a vision, a new way forward that God wants to show you? Will you lean in to listen? God wants to give us a vision that will help dismantle the fears, failures, anxiety, and depression in our lives. Let's courageously and persistently envision what our fears want us to abandon: a beautiful future.

Eleven

A Beautiful Community

"Hey man, can you do me favor? It's for one of our members." I could sense the hesitation in Jason's voice as he asked.

"Uh yeah, what's up?" I replied.

"She is in my office and she's going through a lot, I think she just had a breakdown. Can you talk to her? I hate to ask, but I thought you could help," Jason continued.

"Okay, let me put my stuff down," I told him and headed to the lockers. *And it's the first time I'm actually on time,* I thought to myself. I was going to be early to my CrossFit class for the first time, and now there was this to make me late anyway.

I had discovered the Northlake CrossFit community only a few years prior and loved being part of it. Before Northlake CrossFit, I bounced around to different gyms and training programs. I even trained in Brazilian jujitsu for a while. But it wasn't until CrossFit that I worked out in a gym with no mirrors. At first I thought, *What? No mirrors so I can stare at my amazing self?!* But then I realized that without mirrors, the focus shifts to what you are doing and how you are doing it instead of what you look like working out and who is watching you.

Since we all sort of knew each other from sweating together most days of the week, the word spread that I was a pastor. So, of course, Jason was asking me for help. I walked in and saw a young lady who looked utterly distraught. I had no idea what I was signing myself up for, but looking back now, several years later, I am so glad I said yes.

Her name was Danielle. She started talking right away. Well, she began to talk but could not finish even her first sentence without tears. I quickly realized this was going to be hard for her. And to make it worse, everyone in the gym could see her through the glass wall of the office where we were talking.

"Can I switch seats with you?" I asked. She looked up, momentarily surprised, but then realized what I was doing. Now that her back was to the window, she was able to talk with a little more privacy. She described the abusive relationship she was in and revealed a pattern of other really bad relationships she had found herself in. We talked for an hour, then I asked her to attend a mental health support group at Mosaic Church. I told her if she would commit to going, I would meet her there and stay with her since she had never been to Mosaic. Not only did she show up, but she kept showing up. I encouraged her that she needed a new community if she were going to live a new life.

Danielle submerged herself in community. She committed to a season of therapy, began attending Sunday services, and volunteered at Mosaic. She made new friendships and new priorities. The new people in her life gave her the courage to persist in the

A Beautiful Community   101

battle against her old patterns of life and to find healing from her past trauma.

What God Offers Us

So often we are told that God wants to give us a new life—that if we believe and accept Jesus, we will supernaturally find ourselves in a new life. I'm fully convinced that God moves in unnatural, supernatural ways. But does God give us a new life? Or does God give us a new way to live? This new way to live was embodied by his Son and is empowered by his Spirit. At the end of the day, we have to show up for ourselves. We have to do the work. We have to get our actions to speak louder than the negative voices in our heads. We have to break free from relationships that keep us living out yesterday. We have to live out today to create a better tomorrow. But it can only happen when we're willing to bravely allow other people into our lives.

A beautiful community creates a chrysalis where we can heal from the pains of our past and become a new creation. The church is a beautiful community that I believe at times lies dormant in our faith. When I was introduced to Christianity, I was told that it is a personal faith because we receive a personal salvation and Jesus becomes our personal Lord and Savior. Although I do appreciate God's unique relationship with me, I also know that when I entered into a relationship with Jesus, I did not become a Christian. I became the church.

The beautiful thing about Western culture is that you have the ability to be your own person, to move away from your past. Regardless of where you grew up or which family you were born into, you are not held by those limitations. You can, in one sense, "change your stars"—move up in the world, per se. In Eastern culture, this is a little bit harder to do. Depending on where we were raised, some of us have been limited by our class or our caste. The family we were raised in defined the boundaries within which we could dream and create. That made it hard for a guy like me to move away and break free from my ancestors. But the beautiful thing about Eastern culture is the way those same people can set up your future. Success is not determined by how well an individual does, but by how well his family does. There is a sense of corporate responsibility that says "I move forward if I can make my whole family move forward."

The word *church* is used so many times to refer to a place of worship, but its original intent was to define the people who worship. In the Greek New Testament, the word for church is *ekklēsia*. This word is derived from the Greek word *kaleō* ("to call"), with the prefix *ek* ("out"). In English, the word is translated from the original "called out ones." As the Bible began to get translated, the German word *kirche*, which essentially means "place of worship," was used. This has led to bad theology; it changed the message of Jesus. There is a power to our Christian faith that lies untapped when we fail to be the church—the people of God. The movement of Jesus has always been a cooperative venture. But the culture you were likely raised in causes many people not to see it.

We are familiar with personal responsibility; the concept is necessary, common, ordinary. In Western culture corporate responsibility is the extra to the ordinary and, while it is not common, it is crucial to creating a beautiful world. In case we've forgotten, the goal of Jesus is to create a beautiful world through us. Being the church can also help us walk through rough seasons of doubt, disappointment, and disillusionment. It gives us people to celebrate with in our seasons of hope, joy, and purpose.

A Beautiful Community   103

When the church takes corporate responsibility we create a spiritual home—a safe place for people to love and to be loved. "Home" should be a place where we can grow, be nurtured, discover, and create. Some of us might not have grown up with a safe or healthy home. Home for some of us might be a sad or even painful memory. But we all long for a sense of home. We make "home" with friends as we get older. That's why people say, "These friends are family that I chose."

God created us to live and thrive within a "home," a spiritual family. A beautiful community of people who long to love and lead like Jesus is a beautiful thing. It is a refuge for the hurts, concerns, and even sins of the world. That's why Jesus tells Peter and his disciples, "I will build my church, and the gates of Hades will not overcome it" (Matthew 16:18).

Jesus is painting a beautiful picture of his people, the church—people of the light, standing against hell, which means standing against the darkness. Sin takes us all into the shadows; it makes us go into hiding. It can take us into sunless days and starless nights. As his church, Jesus wants us not only to resist the gates of hell but to break in and rescue people from their darkness.

Forgiveness and Community

Danielle's sexual abuse started in the place she called home. She was just a kid when her uncle started doing terribly inappropriate things with her. But since he was part of her home, he was always around. The home that was supposed to be the safe place for a kid became a fearful and anxious place. As an adult, she left "home." Years later, her uncle was charged with sixty-eight accounts of molestation and rape. He is currently serving 109 years in prison, with no chance for parole.

"So, forgiveness?" I asked Danielle. "How does that work in this situation? Can you even forgive something like this?" I'll never forget her response.

"I have forgiven him," she replied with a confident peace that only comes from deep healing. "I feel bad for him. He used to use the Old Testament stories in the Bible to justify what he would do to us. How messed up do you have to be to believe that?"

Watching people go through something as traumatic as Danielle did leaves us imagining how complicated forgiveness can be. Moving past hurt is hard enough, but when it involves abuse, there are many layers and forgiveness becomes a messy process. It can be a whirlwind of anger, rage, and sadness. You think you're over it and then realize you need to forgive again. It can require a season of therapy and healing. Forgiveness can also be extremely lonely at times because you are left to wrestle with the pain alone. It's you and your opponent. While forgiveness is uniquely experienced, unforgiveness grows into bitterness that can be shared with others. We can divide up our bitterness and resentment among friends and find people to be angry on our behalf. Most of us have people in our lives who will get outraged with us because of what was done to us. But that creates a bitter and divided world.

A beautiful community filled with people who love and care for us can support and strengthen us through hard times. Forgiveness often doesn't remove the sting of what was done to us, but we can harness those feelings away from bitterness into compassion for others.

Bitterness and forgiveness create two different kinds of worlds. Bitterness creates people who want retribution. Forgiveness creates people who want restoration. When we forgive we change and we get better. But we need other people to cheer us on as we

A Beautiful Community 105

enter the ring and fight our demons. That is why we need a beautiful community to surround us. We not only need people who stand with us against oppression, exploitation, harassment, bigotry, and brutality, but we also need people to help forgive, to let go, to absolve, and to acquit an offense. Forgiveness requires friendships, people who will remind us why we have to fight for a better tomorrow. This is one reason we need a beautiful community, a church community.

Jesus and Community

I believe community is one of the reasons Jesus asked his cousin John to baptize him. The baptism of Jesus is one of the rare moments that was recorded in all four Gospels. The story goes that John, slightly overwhelmed, takes Jesus and lowers him into the water of the eastern part of the Jordon River. The site is known as Al-Maghtas, meaning "immersion," but officially known as Baptism Site "Bethany Beyond the Jordan." There are many reasons why Jesus got baptized that day. I think one of the reasons is community. Community? Yes, because baptism happens in a public setting with others because it communicates that we are choosing to belong to a group of people. When we choose to get baptized, among other things, we are declaring our intention of becoming a part of a spiritual community of Jesus. I'm convinced that Jesus was showing us the importance of a beautiful community to belong to.

We cannot grow to become all that God created us to become without others. Think about it: we can't grow in love in a vacuum. Love, which all the commandments hinge on, is tested, refined, and blossoms in relationship with others. Jesus lived to illustrate what God desires. Jesus' baptism shows us that we need one another. This was at the beginning of his earthly ministry. At the end of his earthly ministry, Jesus hung on a cross and said, "Father, forgive them, for they do not know what they are doing" (Luke 23:34). And then John 19:26-27 (NLT) records this: "When Jesus saw his mother standing there beside the disciple he loved, he said to her, 'Dear woman, here is your son.' And he said to this disciple, 'Here is your mother.' And from then on this disciple took her into his home."

Reading these accounts, I can't help but see that forgiveness and community are forever linked. We all need a beautiful Jesus community to empower and encourage us to create a beautiful future. A beautiful community "home" creates a chrysalis where we can heal from the pains of our past and become a new creation.

It was through Danielle's new home, a beautiful church community, that God healed her past home experience. God redeemed what had been an unsafe space with a new home, a place of acceptance, security, and love. A new home that was safe with trustworthy people and supportive friends. It took enormous amounts of courage, patience, and commitment for Danielle to become who she is today. But it would have been impossible for her to heal without a new home.

This home—a beautiful church community—is powerful and complicated. It is powerful because, as Jesus told his disciples, he will give us "the keys of the kingdom of heaven; whatever you bind on earth will be bound in heaven, and whatever you loose on earth will be loosed in heaven" (Matthew 16:19). I'm not going to even try to pretend I know the depth of what Jesus is talking about here. But what if he is saying that we have been given the power to create? What if there is an unseen but inseparable connection between the actions of the church and the activity in heaven?

A Beautiful Community

The church, through its words and actions, creates the world we all live in. Words create worlds; we know this to be true in our lives when we recall what has been spoken over us. Words have either freed us or bound us in life. Jesus ends his thought by telling them "not to tell anyone that he was the Messiah" (Matthew 16:20). It's as if Jesus is saying, "Your time has not yet come. But one day soon you will be my ambassadors. You will be the beautiful people that I will use to heal a broken world" (see 2 Corinthians 5:20).

Church community is complicated because it is made up of people who, like us, are imperfect. That is why we need to explore what true relationships look like. We need to consider the relationships we are in because our friendships forecast our future. Are you ready? Let's go!

Twelve

A Beautiful

Relationship

"I just want you to know that I wouldn't be where I am if it wasn't for you believing in me."

Nurah, my daughter, was in the back seat of the car, but we heard her clearly. I glanced at her to see her facial expression. I knew those words were directed to Ashley, and they meant so much. In fact, those words demolished one of Ashley's biggest worries. Ashley had been homeschooling Nurah and our son, Asher, for a couple of years. She endlessly struggled with her confidence to teach them. She often wondered if she was doing a good job. What made it especially convoluted for Ashley was the reality that Nurah has a learning disability like me. And like me, Nurah struggled with worry and anxiety about her ability to learn.

Both mother and daughter struggled with fear: Nurah in being able to learn and Ashley in being able to teach. But those words created a beautiful moment that disarmed their fear.

A Beautiful Relationship

Beautiful relationships have the power to overcome fear. They fight against feelings of inadequacy in our lives. They help us keep going. They don't let us give up. Our relationships can help us live into God's calling in our lives.

Learning About Diversity

Deep relationships are dynamic. They are continually changing us, for better or worse. They can bring out unseen potential or unforeseen pain in our lives. That is why we have to be intentional about our relationships—the ones that we can choose. Because we can't always choose the people who will be around us.

It has been estimated that the average person will spend one-third of their life at work. That is a lot of time with people that we didn't necessarily get to choose. My first job was volunteering at a local hospital. It was months after Kuwait got liberated from Iraq. I was sixteen years old and worked in the food service department. I just wanted to help my community, so I thought the hospital would be a good place to start. I did not realize that experience would expose me to the cruelties of war up close.

Delivering food to some of these patients was rough. I learned how their diet determined whether they were getting better. Working at a hospital indeed shaped my worldview, but working with the hospital staff shaped my character. As of 2022, Kuwait has a population of 4.45 million people, of which 1.45 million are Kuwaiti citizens. The remaining 3 million are foreign nationals from more than 100 countries. I worked with Arab nurses, Indian shift managers, and a Filipino department head. Spending time with these beautifully diverse people profoundly cemented in me the uniqueness and importance of cultures.

Learning to Stand Against Injustice

I met Jake when I was working in a restaurant. He was the manager, a passionate Filipino who was pretty strict but also kind and generous. In this job, I learned the value of working hard, partly because Jake did not give me any leeway. In fact, I disliked him my first week of working there, but quickly I began to respect him. He taught me so many things, one of which was to stand up against injustice and prejudice.

Racism and prejudice were rampant and apparent in Kuwait in the 1990s. The most privileged people were the Kuwaitis. Then it was Arabs in general, then Muslims, and then everybody else. My manager, a Filipino, fell on the lower end of totem pole.

The restaurant that we worked at had a shuttle bus that would take people home on certain days. On one particular day we were all on the bus to be dropped off to our homes. There were all different kinds of people on the bus. The driver decided to drop off all the Muslims and Arabs first, even though the majority of Filipinos and Indians lived close. We did not know what he was doing until we noticed that he was driving past the homes of certain people on the bus to give priority to the Muslims and Arabs.

I saw it happen, but I didn't know what I should do. That was when Jake said something. He asked the driver what he was doing, and the response he got was that he was a Filipino so he would have to wait. Jake asked the driver to stop the bus, which caused a scene. At first the driver ignored him, but as Jake got louder, the driver got louder as well. Jake got up from his seat, walked up to the driver, and insisted that he stop the bus. I can still remember that scene. He told the driver that he was not going to stand there and be treated with prejudice. Jake told him that what he was doing

A Beautiful Relationship 111

was wrong, and he refused to be treated that way. Jake walked off the bus right there.

I so badly wanted to join him. There was something inside of me that knew that what Jake was doing was right. Unfortunately, I was just a kid and didn't know what I would do if I got off the bus. It's not like we had Uber or Lyft back in those days. Jake would have to walk or hitchhike to get home. But he did it. The next week things changed. The driver was told to drop people off based on their location and not their ethnicity. I will never forget that incident because that day Jake showed me how to courageously stand up to inequality.

I'm so glad to have known him; having had so many insightful conversations and incredible experiences shaped my worldview. His friendship taught me to appreciate the beauty of diversity of thought and culture. My relationship with Jake was one of the beautiful ones that stuck with me and has empowered me to stand up for what's right.

Decades later, I found myself in a conversation with someone who asked me to speak at a citywide protest against police brutality in our city. I had already helped him organize the first of many nonviolent protests that had begun to take shape after the death of George Floyd. Our church had helped organize this event, and we had close to 3,000 people show up in the heart of our city, Charlotte, North Carolina. I knew it was the right thing to do as an individual but also as the church.

"I'm not quite sure if I'm qualified to speak. I am a Pakistani, immigrant pastor, bro."

"That is why you need to speak," he said. He was not taking no for an answer.

So I did. I spoke vulnerably and honestly to the crowd about my insecurity of addressing them. I told them that I did not feel worthy to talk to them because of who I was. But then, I reminded myself and them that this fight against injustice was a fight for love against hate. It was not a fight of one race against another, one kind of people against another kind of people. It was truly a fight against prejudice, hatred, and injustice against anyone. And our weapon was love.

I told them that, at the end of the day, what's most important is that we are for love and our fight is against hate. Regardless of where they saw themselves in the middle of this conflict in culture, I urged them to fight for love and with love.

People thanked me for my words, but I couldn't help but be so thankful for the *relationships in my life that prepared me to step into the moment.*

I am convinced that if you have beautiful relationships, they will help you conquer your deepest fears and insecurities. These beautiful relationships can be friendships and partnerships. They can be found in the context of a family, a friend group, a marriage, a church community, or even a fitness community. Beautiful relationships are not easy, but they are worth developing and fighting for. These relationships can become incubators of your character and your potential, creating ideal environments for you to mature and grow.

God Speaks Through Our Relationships

These beautiful relationships are God-sent, for God uses them to speak to you. Their words at times can be God's word to you in the exact moment you need to hear them. *Chronos* is a Greek word for quantitative or linear time. It's the root of the word "chronological," meaning when we're thinking of time in a particular order. But

A Beautiful Relationship 113

kairos times are divine moments in time. God sets up *kairos* moments for us in these beautiful relationships so we can know that God is speaking through other people to us. The words pierce our hearts and comfort our souls because they are from God himself.

The beautiful relationships in our lives will help us conquer our biggest fears and may even awaken our heroic selves. We've seen this play out in movies in which people willingly expose themselves to risk and danger because of the people they love. There always seems to be a moment in which the protagonist decides to become the hero because of the people in their life who need them.

This plays out not only in fictional stories but also in real life. You might know a person in your life who propelled you to become more than you thought you were. They accepted who you were; they truly saw who you were and also who you could become. They are the people you would likely do anything for—not because you are capable of anything, but because of your relationship with them, you're willing to do whatever it takes. It could be a close friend, a beloved spouse, or your precious kids who give you the power to push past your fear and insecurity to wrestle your inner demons and do the seemingly impossible.

Jesus and John the Baptist

When John the Baptist is imprisoned and waiting to be executed, he sends word to Jesus and the disciples. John asks, "Are you the Messiah we've been expecting, or should we keep looking for someone else?" (Matthew 11:3 NLT). It would seem that John is questioning whether Jesus is the Messiah. But it doesn't add up, especially when we know that John was the guy who baptized Jesus and called him the Lamb of God who would take away the sins of the world.

114 PART THREE: TOMORROW NEEDS YOU

John was also Jesus' cousin, so we can only imagine that they grew up together. Even Elizabeth, John's mother, knew early on in her pregnancy with John that Mary's virgin birth of Jesus was the beginning of something different. John was the forerunner before Jesus. He lived his entire life, "preparing the way" for Jesus. So he wasn't asking this question in the prison because he did not know who the Messiah was. He had spent his whole life preparing the way for his cousin Jesus to be revealed as the Messiah. So what was John really asking here? What John is asking is revealed by Jesus' answer:

> Jesus told them, "Go back to John and tell him what you have heard and seen—the blind see, the lame walk, those with leprosy are cured, the deaf hear, the dead are raised to life, and the Good News is being preached to the poor." And he added, "God blesses those who do not fall away because of me." (Matthew 11:4-6 NLT)

It seems to me that Jesus is sending John a message: "I'm the one, the one who has the power to perform supernatural miracles, and I have saved others but I'm not coming to save you."

And John might be wondering of Jesus, *Is this how I'm going to die for you? I've lived my whole life for you and now I'm waiting to be executed. I just want to know if my life mattered and, if I did, what I was supposed to do.* This interaction reveals a beautiful, deep relationship that Jesus had with John. Jesus was reminding John that he had indeed prepared the way of Jesus and, in doing so, changed people's lives. Jesus seems to be saying, it's because of what you did that I can now do what I need to do.

John spent his life baptizing and creating disciples for Jesus and then, after baptizing Jesus, told them to go follow him. Jesus and

A Beautiful Relationship   115

John never did ministry together. John didn't become a disciple of Jesus. It seems like John was called to more, to go before, to lead, to prepare the way for Jesus' purpose. (In case you were wondering, at one time I too thought this story was about John, a disciple of Jesus. However, it is about another John—John the Baptist.)

John put the beautiful relationship he had with Jesus before him and, because of it, was able to do incredible things with his life. He was able to live a single, focused life in the desert, surviving on almost nothing, doing hard things. He was ridiculed, misunderstood, and mistreated because he had set his relationship with Jesus before him, even when people didn't understand why. This empowerment allowed John to be more courageous than he could ever be, to the point of boldly facing death because John knew it would be worth it. His life would have meaning. He would play a part in introducing Jesus who would change the world as they knew it. We need these kinds of relationships in our lives to empower us to do more and be more. Relationships in which we encourage and are encouraged.

After he told the messengers what to tell John, Jesus turned and told his disciples about John:

> What kind of man did you go into the wilderness to see? Was he a weak reed, swayed by every breath of wind? Or were you expecting to see a man dressed in expensive clothes? No, people with expensive clothes live in palaces. Were you looking for a prophet? Yes, and he is more than a prophet. John is the man to whom the Scriptures refer when they say,
>
> > "Look, I am sending my messenger ahead of you,
> > and he will prepare your way before you."
> > (Matthew 11:7-10 NLT)

116 PART THREE: TOMORROW NEEDS YOU

And then he tells them: "I tell you the truth, of all who have ever lived, none is greater than John the Baptist. Yet even the least person in the kingdom of heaven is greater than he is!" (Matthew 11:11 NLT).

Essentially, Jesus was saying, "I know John like no one else does. He's not a guy who ever sought to live a life of privilege and power. Nor was John too precious to get his hand dirty. John is the guy who lived his life for me, and now he's going to die for me. I know that I can go save him. I could just say the word and the prison doors would open wide and he could walk right out. But that's not the plan. John understands that there are bigger things at play. John is a man who is not going to be offended because I do not show up the way people expect me to show up. John is someone who has a beautiful relationship with me that goes beyond the surface. Relationships like this are deep and rich, and they can stand an immense amount of stress and anxiety."

The relationship that John had with Jesus is one that Jesus is offering to you as well. If you doubt you could ever be like John, or you know you are nothing like him, I'm telling you that if you would do what John did—if you would set a beautiful relationship with Jesus before you—you will do even greater things than John the Baptist.

So, we have to ask ourselves two questions. First, do we have beautiful relationships in our lives that fortify us as we fight our fears? Second, do we have a relationship with Jesus, a beautiful friendship that makes us fierce?

Thirteen

The Broken Creating

Beauty

"It hurts to be in this world. I saw the pain every time I looked at my dad's and mom's faces. I'm such a wreck and piece of trash. The world would be so much better if I was not in it. It would help everybody. I was so much of a screwup, and life would be so much better for everybody else if I wasn't in this world. So yes, I did; I did load one bullet into the chamber, point it to my head, and squeeze the trigger."

I could not believe what I was hearing. This was John Mark Redwine, a pastor of the Gathering Church in Asheville, North Carolina. He was recalling a moment in his life that led to truly meeting Jesus for the very first time. "I started getting bullied early on in youth group and just believed that I would never amount to much. I didn't have much self-worth, and I just longed to be free from the anxiety for so long. So right after high school, I enrolled in the Coast Guard. I believed that joining the military was going to make me matter in life, give me purpose. I just did not want to be a screwup."

PART THREE: TOMORROW NEEDS YOU

I could see it in his face as John Mark recounted his pain and trauma. "I saw too much in the Coast Guard. Right after boot camp, I went into specialist training and became a gunner mate and then was given my first unit on a Coast Guard Cutter," he continued.

"Being so young, barely twenty-one years old, I saw too much. I saw the worst of humanity—from human trafficking to pulling out dead bodies from the sea, confronting drug dealers to catching Haitian and Cuban immigrants trying to get to the United States. It just got to be too much. Even though I was trying to serve my country, it did not give me the peace and purpose I was trying to find."

"So what did you do?" I asked him. He told me that he started drinking a whole lot, chain smoking, and finding any way to cope with the pain and the torment that he faced waking up every day.

"Yeah, so the gun misfired," he said, alarmed and grateful.

"What did you do after that?" I asked.

"Well, I didn't know what to think. I was just overwhelmed by that moment, and I didn't know what was happening because it's very rare for a gun to misfire. I sobbed myself to sleep that night. But the next morning I woke up thinking about if I should try again."

"Did you?" I hesitated as I asked.

"I was going to. I had a plan," he told me. He explained that he was going to be deployed for about ninety days and that after he came back he was going to try again, but this time make sure that the gun was fully loaded. However, right before he got deployed the phone rang.

It was his wife, Rahel. She called to say, "I can tell something is wrong with you. You are broken, lost, and searching for peace and

The Broken Creating Beauty

purpose in all the wrong places. The only peace in life you will find is in a relationship with Jesus."

"I always thought God was a bully. He had high expectations that no one really could meet. I never thought God wanted a friendship with me," John Mark blurted out, as he thought back to what Rahel had said. "And I knew she was right; so I went and found a Gideon Bible and began reading it."

John Mark read the entire Bible in about a month and a half. He still struggled with thoughts of suicide and still smoked constantly, but something changed that day. He gave his "broken" life to Jesus and began to see how God was going to make him "beautiful." He told me that even though he woke up with all kinds of negative thoughts, he also woke up with hope, which is the one thing we cannot live without as humans. Previously, when depression asked him if he was worthy or if he was loved, he didn't think he was. But after he entered into a relationship with Jesus, he found an answer for both of those questions. He enrolled in online seminary and eventually got his master's degree and then planted the Gathering in 2015 in Asheville, North Carolina.

John Mark Redwine is one of many people who have found a deep sense of meaning through a beautiful relationship with Jesus. Trusting Jesus doesn't mean we will never struggle, as John Mark acknowledges: "Even now I have to put my relationship with Jesus and my relationships with my family before me to overcome intense anxiety and depression in my life." He told me that if it weren't for those beautiful people it would be very hard to fight off the inner demons that want to drag him into hopelessness and depression. He told me it's a choice that he has to make every day to put those beautiful things before him, and those could not be fulfilled if he didn't have a beautiful relationship with Jesus. A relationship that allows him to be himself, that doesn't ask him to be anybody else. A relationship that offers acceptance, grace, and love. A relationship that challenges him to be more than he thinks he could be, and to realize the potential that God had created within him.

You might not have a story like that of John Mark, but your pain and your past are real. I'm convinced that we have to put something so beautiful in front of us because it's the only thing that will allow us to overcome and fight the fear and anxiety, the distress and hopelessness in our lives. God is inviting you to have a beautiful relationship with him.

Maybe you did not grow up with the possibility of a relationship with God. Maybe the idea of a friendship with God is absurd to you. It was to me. Can God be a friend? Jesus seems to think so: "I call you friends, because I have told you everything I heard from my Father" (John 15:15 GNT).

Discovering God as My Friend

One of my fondest childhood memories is staying up all night with my older brother during the month of Ramadan. Ramadan is a period of time in the ninth month of the Islamic calendar observed by Muslims worldwide as a month of fasting, prayer, reflection, and community. We would eat our meal right before dawn and perform our first Salat, a Muslim ritual prayer, one of five in a day. After the prayer, we would leave our house to ride our bicycles on the streets as the sun was coming up. I still remember the air so clean and crisp, the smell of jasmine flowers everywhere. Life was simple back then. God was simple back then, too.

But life and God got complicated as I got older. I started wondering if my relationship with Allah, the God of Islam, was as good

The Broken Creating Beauty

as it was going to get. My relationship with Allah was mostly on a Janamaz, a prayer rug. On this rug, I would perform my Salat prayers. But first, I had to perform the Wudhu, a ceremonial cleanse that involves washing by rubbing several parts of the body three times while saying Bismillah ("in the name of Allah"). After the Wudhu, I would lay my Janamaz down in a particular direction called Qiblah, the fixed direction toward the Ka'bah, the Grand Mosque in Makkah, Saudi Arabia. It's the direction all Muslims face when performing their prayers, no matter where they are in the world.

Then I began to recite passages from the Qur'an in Arabic, which is the only language they are permitted to be recited in. At the end of these ritual prayers, we were allowed to make personal requests in our language before we folded up our rugs. This was the depth of my relationship with Allah. There would be times when I would plead with Allah to help me, but I knew that these weren't valid prayers since they were not in Arabic. Reading the Qur'an had its own challenges. Most Muslims memorize sections of the Qur'an so they can recite it but rarely understand what it means. The Qur'an is complicated and also considered very holy. To read the Qur'an, I had to perform the same routines as when I did my prayers.

Needless to say, connecting with Allah was a process. He was holy, and to be in his presence you had to clean up who you were. Although I see the sincerity in the sacraments that gave me access to Allah, I never felt connected with him. How could I? The relationship was formal, impersonal, and transactional. I needed him to meet my needs, so I was committed to meet his requirements. That was the deal. I never thought there could be more to my relationship with God.

But, as I shared in chapter three, it all changed one night when I met Jesus in my room.

It was at Fellowship of Christian Athletes (FCA) where I first heard about a God who is personal, a God who is pursuing us and wants to be with us. My brother and his friends talked about the "good news" that Jesus was God incarnate, stepping into human history to redeem and reconcile us back to God. They shared a new idea that God didn't need to be worshiped in temples and with ceremony. Jesus talked about worshiping God in spirit and in truth, removing any kind of rituals that people needed to perform. They said that we have an open-heaven relationship and that God made our bodies the new temple for his Spirit to dwell in. One night at FCA I remember thinking to myself, *I wonder if what they're talking about could be true.*

Three nights later I encountered the demon and ran to my brother in terror. Mahmood said: "There's only one person I know who has authority over demons and angels."

"Who?" I asked eagerly.

"Jesus," he replied.

"Well, okay. Then let's do this," I said, now ready to do whatever it took for him to help me.

My brother Mahmood told me he was going to lead me in a prayer to accept Jesus, and asked me to repeat after him. But before he began I asked if I could say something to Jesus.

"Jesus, I don't know who you are so I can't call you the Lord of my life. I can't say I love you because I don't know you. But if you will save me from this, I will give you my whole life." These words were the beginning of my beautiful relationship with Jesus.

Then we prayed together, and Mahmood ended with saying "Amen." As I opened my eyes, I could see the joy and excitement in

The Broken Creating Beauty

his face. He was thrilled by what had happened. I, however, was still scared to death, so I hinted that I would be sleeping beside him. But Mahmood quickly challenged me to go back in my room. He gave me a New Testament Gideon Bible that was smaller than an iPhone. It was the first Bible I had held, and I was wondering if it was made for Hobbits. But seriously, I had no intention of going back into that room. I thought a better plan was to spoon my brother for a couple of weeks. Finally, he dared me to go back to my room, and I did. I turned on all the lights, sat up in my bed, and began reading the Bible. Have you noticed that when you are terrified and spooked that everything makes a sound? An hour into it, exhausted and frustrated, I shut off the lights, sat in my bed, and looked up and said, "Jesus, if I die tonight, it is your fault."

Shortly after I had pulled the covers over my head and got into a fetal position, I felt something try to wake me. I found myself sitting on my bed with my eyes open, staring into a presence that I can't really understand or explain. I have never felt peace so aggressive. There he was—Jesus. I was looking at him, but I was inside of him at the same time. I was not quite sure what I was seeing; his presence was so intoxicating. I couldn't keep my eyes off him, but I couldn't keep my eyes open.

Friendship with Jesus

"I am Jesus, and your life is not your own." I will never forget those words. Those words were the beginning of a friendship that has lasted all these years. This friendship of Jesus has been with me through so much pain and trauma, as I've witnessed incredible miracles and experienced overwhelming joy. This friendship allowed me to lead my two sisters to know Jesus and also my dad before he passed.

I can only imagine your past and the pain associated with it. I can only speculate how traumatic it was because I was not there to experience it the way you did. I can only empathize with your story; I can't fully comprehend the depth of your struggle. But I do know one who can. His name is Jesus. "For we do not have a high priest who is unable to empathize with our weaknesses, but we have one who has been tempted in every way, just as we are—yet he did not sin" (Hebrews 4:15).

Jesus has been with you throughout your whole life. Like me, you probably did not notice his presence and his pursuit of you, but I can assure you he's been with you this whole time. He was with you when you were betrayed, abused, and abandoned. He was there when you felt all alone, ashamed, and vulnerable. He has been there at the high points of your life and the lowest lows of your life.

We have been told to follow Jesus, but Jesus doesn't want just followers; he wants friends. He's not a god who wants to bulldoze your plans in life but, rather, he wants to partner with you to fulfill your purpose. A beautiful friendship with Jesus demolishes all the fears in our lives.

Unqualified but Called

"How could God ever use me?" "How could I be someone who could be part of something so amazing?" "I don't have what it takes." "I'm not as good as people think I am." "I could never do that." "I'm nobody." "No one's going to follow me." "There are already people doing it, and doing it so much better." "People are gonna think I'm stupid." "It's impossible for a person like me." "There are too many things against me." "I don't have a good history."

King David, who is attributed as writing most of the book of Psalms, asked the same questions when he wrote:

The Broken Creating Beauty

When I look at the night sky and see the work of your fingers—
 the moon and the stars you set in place—
what are mere mortals that you should think about them,
 human beings that you should care for them?
 (Psalm 8:3-4 NLT)

Have you ever had thoughts like these? I have. I occasionally still wrestle with them. It's so hard for me to fathom that a guy like me could be used by an amazing God. But the more time I spend in a relationship with Jesus, the more I am able to see that God truly knows me fully, loves me completely, and has chosen me undoubtedly.

"Crooked sticks draw straight lines." This lyrical line from one of Lecrae's songs suggests that God uses imperfect people to accomplish his perfect will. That would also mean that God does not wait for us to be good before using us to do good. God uses us to transform the world as he is conforming us into the image of his Son.

This should not be a surprise to us if we are familiar with the Bible, this library of books that has so many stories of God choosing flawed people to further his kingdom. In fact, starting with Adam and Eve in Genesis (the first book) and continuing to Revelation (the last book), there is "dirt" on every person God uses in both the Old and New Testaments. I'm so thankful for this because I'm as sinful as they get. In spite of my choices, time after time, God has used me to help and heal people. I believe if I'm honest with God, he will make me holy. But if I only pretend to be holy, I'm never truly honest.

If you've ever wondered what God thinks of you and whether he could use you, I want you to know this: God knows that you are a sinner, and he knows what he is working with. He loves you and wants you to serve him just as you are. All he wants is for you to be honest with yourself and with him by confessing your sin and following him. He will take care of the rest.

Jesus said, "I am the vine; you are the branches. If you remain in me and I in you, you will bear much fruit; apart from me you can do nothing" (John 15:5). God's intention has always been to work in us, with us, and through us. It seems like we were created with that in mind.

Is your yesterday keeping you from engaging today? Is it trying to convince you that tomorrow doesn't need you? I pray you realize that, regardless of a traumatic and tragic past, you can begin to use the beautiful things in your life to create an amazing future. I pray that you do not believe the lie that your yesterday defines you. I pray you realize that you are not bound to your yesterdays. I pray you resist the temptation to waste today. I pray that you don't get disheartened and begin to disengage from what you need to do today. I pray you will be convinced that God is calling you into the beautiful opportunities and relationships he has for your life. Tomorrow needs you.

Acknowledgments

To my family, you love me more than I deserve. Ashley, I can't see my world without you, my love. Asher, your words have put immense courage in me. Nurah, your presence empowers me to do hard things. I can't imagine how I would have finished this project without all of you.

To my childhood family, I stand today on your love and sacrifice. To Atiya, my sweet little sister, you are one of the strongest women I know. Your deep love of Jesus has saved me so many times.

To my friends, I'm beyond grateful to you for keeping me sane during this project! Thank you for genuine excitement and sincere prayers.

To Mosaic, my Jesus community, you are my muse. You are living proof of the broken creating beauty.

To Kristin, I don't have the words; you know this since you literally helped me write this book! Thank you for believing in me, working with me every step of the way. Thank you for being in my life all these years. So profoundly grateful for you, my friend.

To the incredibly brave people who allowed me to share their powerful stories, you inspire me. Thank you for trusting me with your past. Your resilience will rescue our world.

130   *Acknowledgments*

To Alex and the Bindery team, thank you for taking a chance on me.

To Cindy, Rachel, and everyone on the InterVarsity Press team, thank you for being so kind and patient with me.

To Regina, the prayer warrior who moonlights as a writing coach, thank you for "birthing this baby."

Notes

2. Learning to Trust God Again

16 *We did that day:* I go into the details of this in my book *Ex-Muslim* (Nashville, TN: Thomas Nelson, 2022).

21 *Develops when a person:* Substance Abuse and Mental Health Services Administration, "Post-Traumatic Stress Disorder (PTSD)," April 24, 2023, www.samhsa.gov/mental-health/post-traumatic-stress-disorder?scrlybrkr=f4e0a113.

PTG is the "positive change": College of Humanities and Earth and Social Sciences, University of North Carolina, Charlotte, "UNC Charlotte's Posttraumatic Growth Research Continues to Influence," December 5, 2015, https://chess.charlotte.edu/2015/12/05/unc-charlottes-posttraumatic-growth-research-continues-to-influence/.

22 *new systematic study of PTG by professionals:* Boulder Crest Foundation, "Understanding Posttraumatic Growth," Boulder Crest Foundation, 2024, https://bouldercrest.org/research-resources/what-is-posttraumatic-growth-ptg.

Five domains of posttraumatic growth: Josh Goldberg, "The Five Domains of PTG," Boulder Crest Foundation, August 25, 2023, https://bouldercrest.org/research-resources/what-is-posttraumatic-growth-ptg/discover-the-domains-of-ptg.

3. My Relationship with Fear

31 *As soon as you recognize fear:* "5 Things You Never Knew About Fear," Northwestern Medicine, October 2020, www.nm.org/healthbeat/healthy-tips/emotional-health/5-things-you-never-knew-about-fear.

31 *During a staged fear:* "5 Things You Never Knew."
32 *Taking drastic measures:* "5 Things You Never Knew."

4. Fear of Loss

42 *"No pessimist":* Helen Keller, *Optimism* (1903), "Part III: The Practice of Optimism," transcription, American Foundation for the Blind, https://afb .org/about-afb/history/helen-keller/books-essays-speeches/optimism -1903.

5. Fear of Failure

47 *This kind of anxiety:* Paul Ekman Group, "Fear," accessed September 16, 2024, www.paulekman.com/universal-emotions/what-is-fear.

6. Fear of Rejection

60 *Brain imaging research:* Naomi I. Eisenberger, "Social Pain and the Brain: Controversies, Questions, and Where to Go from Here," *Annual Review of Psychology* 66 (2015): 601-29, https://www.annualreviews.org/content /journals/10.1146/annurev-psych-010213-115146.

8. Why Beauty?

74 *"Our ability to reach unity in diversity":* Mahatma Gandhi, *Young India 1924–1926* (Triplicane, Madras, S.E., India: S. Ganesan, 1927), 464, www. google.com/books/edition/Young_India_1924_1926/-bscAAAAMAAJ?hl =en&gbpv=0.

75 *"Beauty changed them":* Thomas Peschak, "Dive into an Ocean Photographer's World," TED, October 2015, www.ted.com/talks/thomas_peschak _dive_into_an_ocean_photographer_s_world?referrer=playlist-reconnect _with_nature&autoplay=true.

9. What Do You See?

81 *Basic explanation:* Wikipedia, s.v., "evil eye," last modified October 11, 2024, https://en.wikipedia.org/wiki/Evil_eye.

10. A Beautiful Vision

90 *A beautiful vision:* I talk about this experience in my book *Ex-Muslim* (Nashville, TN: Thomas Nelson, 2022).

95 *Three different exiles:* "Exile to Babylon," *ESV Global Study Bible,* www.esv.org/resources/esv-global-study-bible/map-14-16.
Job, an upright man: Richard Hooker, "The Hebrews: A Learning Module," Washington State University.